Everything You Need to Know

Introduction: Discovering the Islands of Fiji

Welcome to the enchanting paradise of Fiji, where turquoise waters, pristine beaches, and lush green landscapes come together to create a tropical haven like no other. Nestled in the heart of the South Pacific Ocean, Fiji is an archipelago comprising over 300 islands, each with its own unique charm and character. As we embark on this journey of discovery, let us immerse ourselves in the rich history, captivating culture, and breathtaking natural beauty that define this mesmerizing destination.

Fiji's history traces back thousands of years, with evidence of early settlement by the Lapita people around 1500 BCE. These skilled navigators and artisans laid the foundation for the vibrant Fijian culture we witness today. Over the centuries, the islands witnessed waves of migration and interactions with neighboring communities, including Polynesians, Europeans, and Asians. The islands' diverse heritage is a tapestry woven from these various influences, each contributing to the colorful and fascinating cultural landscape of Fiji.

The Fijian archipelago is divided into two main groups: the larger Viti Levu, home to the capital city, Suva, and the smaller Vanua Levu, which boasts a more tranquil and off-the-beaten-path experience. Beyond these major islands, there are several other smaller gems, such as Taveuni, known as the "Garden Island" for its lush vegetation, and the Mamanuca and Yasawa Islands, famous for their idyllic resorts and sandy shores.

While Fiji is celebrated for its natural beauty, the warm-hearted and welcoming locals, known as Fijians, are its true treasures. The traditional village life remains an integral part of the Fijian identity, where communal living, respect for elders, and a strong sense of community bond are cherished values. Visitors are often invited to partake in the traditional Kava ceremony, a symbol of friendship and respect, where a local drink made from the Kava root is shared as a gesture of welcome.

One of the most remarkable aspects of Fiji is its resilience and ability to preserve its unique customs and traditions amidst the waves of modernity. The preservation of the indigenous Fijian language, along with the celebration of traditional arts and crafts, such as wood carving, weaving, and pottery, is a testament to the islanders' deep-rooted cultural pride.

Beyond the captivating culture, Fiji's natural wonders beckon travelers from around the globe. The Coral Coast on the southern shores of Viti Levu boasts spectacular coral reefs teeming with marine life, offering an underwater paradise for snorkelers and divers. The Yasawa Islands, with their limestone cliffs and hidden caves, provide a sense of untouched beauty that feels like stepping into a postcard.

As we venture into the heart of Fiji's dense rainforests, we discover an array of endemic plant and animal species, some found nowhere else on Earth. From the vibrant Orange Dove and the rare Crested Iguana to the striking Fiji Banded Iguana, these creatures epitomize the unique biodiversity that thrives within this ecological haven.

Fiji's warm tropical climate is characterized by two distinct seasons - the wet season from November to April and the dry season from May to October. The summer months bring occasional tropical storms, but they are usually short-lived, quickly replaced by bright sunny days, perfect for basking on the sandy shores.

Whether you seek an adventure-packed holiday exploring the rugged terrains, a serene escape to remote islands, or a cultural immersion into the heart of Fijian traditions, this extraordinary archipelago offers an abundance of experiences that cater to every traveler's desires.

In this book, we will delve deeper into Fiji's history, from its ancient origins to its colonial past, and explore the most captivating aspects of its wildlife, cuisine, and cultural heritage. We will uncover the hidden gems of Fiji's cities and immerse ourselves in the vibrant and diverse communities that make this place truly magical.

So, let the journey begin, and let Fiji's allure envelop your senses as we uncover the secrets and wonders of this extraordinary destination. Welcome to Fiji – where paradise awaits!

Unveiling Fiji's Rich History

In the heart of the South Pacific lies Fiji, a land with a history as fascinating as its turquoise waters. Unraveling the past of this island paradise reveals a tapestry woven with the threads of ancient civilizations, colonization, struggles for independence, and the eventual emergence of a modern nation.

The story of Fiji begins with the arrival of the Lapita people around 1500 BCE. These skilled navigators and seafarers settled in the islands, leaving behind intricate pottery and artifacts that provide insights into their way of life. Over the centuries, Fiji became a hub of trade and cultural exchange, as Polynesians, Melanesians, and even some Micronesian communities found their way to these tropical shores.

As the European exploration of the Pacific commenced, the 17th and 18th centuries saw the likes of Abel Tasman and Captain James Cook charting the waters around Fiji. However, it wasn't until the 19th century that Europeans took a more significant interest in the islands. Missionaries arrived, bringing Christianity, and soon after, European traders and adventurers followed.

The mid-19th century saw Fiji plunged into a turbulent era with the advent of the "blackbirding" period, where thousands of laborers, mostly from India and the Pacific, were brought in to work on sugarcane plantations. This dark chapter in Fiji's history marked the beginning of a new socio-economic landscape and shaped the multicultural fabric of the nation.

In 1874, Fiji officially became a British colony, and British governors were appointed to rule the islands. During this period, the economy thrived on sugarcane exports, but it also faced challenges related to labor rights and land ownership, leading to tensions between the indigenous Fijians and the growing Indo-Fijian population.

As the 20th century dawned, Fijian nationalism began to stir, and demands for self-governance grew stronger. It was not until 1970 that Fiji gained independence from British colonial rule, and Ratu Sir Kamisese Mara became its first Prime Minister.

In the decades following independence, Fiji faced internal struggles and political instability. The coups of 1987, driven by ethnic tensions, shook the nation and led to complex questions surrounding democracy and representation. Subsequent coups in 2000 further compounded these challenges.

However, amidst these upheavals, Fiji gradually paved its way towards a more stable and inclusive society. The Fijian government focused on nation-building, fostering a sense of unity and common identity among its diverse population.

In 1987, Fiji adopted a new constitution that recognized the equal status of all citizens, irrespective of ethnicity, and emphasized the concept of a multiracial nation. This commitment to inclusivity was further solidified in the 2013 constitution, which aimed to ensure a fair representation of all communities in the government.

Modern Fiji has emerged as a parliamentary democracy with a President as the Head of State and a Prime Minister as the Head of Government. The nation's political landscape continues to evolve, reflecting the aspirations and desires of its people for a united, prosperous, and peaceful future.

Today, Fiji stands as a thriving nation, boasting a growing economy driven by tourism, agriculture, and manufacturing industries. Its pristine beaches, vibrant culture, and warm hospitality attract visitors from all corners of the world, making tourism a vital contributor to the nation's growth.

As we uncover Fiji's rich history, we come to understand the resilience and strength of its people, who have navigated through tumultuous times to forge a unique identity that embraces diversity. The ancient spirits of the Lapita people, the echoes of colonial times, and the determination for self-governance converge to create the vibrant mosaic that is Fiji.

Pre-Colonial Fiji: A Glimpse into Ancient Civilizations

Long before the first European explorers set foot on Fiji's shores, this enchanting archipelago was already home to thriving ancient civilizations. The pre-colonial era of Fiji's history holds a wealth of secrets and marvels that provide us with a fascinating glimpse into the lives of its early inhabitants.

Around 1500 BCE, the Lapita people, skilled navigators and seafarers, arrived in Fiji after a remarkable voyage across the Pacific Ocean. They settled on various islands, including Viti Levu and Vanua Levu, leaving behind a legacy of distinctive pottery and artifacts. These early settlers established coastal communities, cultivating the fertile lands and utilizing the rich marine resources of the surrounding waters.

The Lapita culture was characterized by intricate designs on their pottery, reflecting their craftsmanship and artistic sensibilities. Their society thrived on fishing, agriculture, and hunting, and they lived in close harmony with nature, embracing the bounties it offered.

As centuries passed, Fiji's pre-colonial era witnessed the arrival of more migrants from different parts of the Pacific. Polynesians and Melanesians added their influences to the cultural tapestry, further enriching the diversity of the islands.

The ancient Fijians developed a complex social structure centered around kinship ties and communal living. Clans and tribes formed the building blocks of society, each with its own unique traditions and customs. Chiefs held significant authority and played crucial roles in maintaining order and resolving disputes within their communities.

The traditional Fijian religion revolved around animism, where spirits were believed to inhabit natural elements such as rocks, trees, and rivers. The ancestral spirits were revered and offered prayers and offerings for protection and blessings. The practice of tabu (or tapu) held immense importance, signifying areas or objects that were sacred or restricted.

Warfare was an integral part of pre-colonial Fijian society. Chiefs and warriors engaged in battles over resources, land, and occasionally, for prestige. The use of war clubs, spears, and other traditional weapons showcased the skills and prowess of these fierce warriors.

One of the most significant cultural aspects of pre-colonial Fiji was the oral tradition. The art of storytelling and song was a means of passing down historical accounts, myths, legends, and genealogies from one generation to another. These oral traditions provided a valuable link to the past and offered insights into the beliefs and experiences of ancient Fijians.

In addition to their mastery in pottery, ancient Fijians were skilled craftsmen, producing intricate wooden carvings, exquisite woven mats, and finely-crafted canoes. These artisanal creations served both practical and ceremonial purposes, showcasing their creativity and artistic flair.

Trade played a vital role in connecting Fiji with neighboring islands. The exchange of goods, including precious stones, shells, and food items, facilitated cultural interactions and created networks of alliances.

The ancient Fijians' connection with the natural world was profound. The reverence for nature, expressed through various ceremonies and rituals, underscored their deep spiritual beliefs and their understanding of the interconnectedness between humans and their environment.

As we explore the pre-colonial era of Fiji's history, we gain a glimpse into a time when the islands were a thriving tapestry of cultures, traditions, and societies. The legacy of the Lapita people, the influences of Polynesians and Melanesians, and the complex social structures of ancient Fijian clans collectively contributed to shaping the identity and heritage of the modern Fijian nation.

Arrival of Europeans and Colonial Era

As the sun set on the pre-colonial era of Fiji, a new chapter in the island's history was about to unfold. The arrival of European explorers in the 17th and 18th centuries marked the beginning of a transformative period that would shape Fiji's destiny for centuries to come.

In 1643, Dutch explorer Abel Tasman became one of the first Europeans to set eyes on the islands of Fiji during his voyage through the Pacific. However, it was not until the late 18th century that the famous British explorer, Captain James Cook, navigated the waters of the South Pacific and visited the Fijian archipelago in 1774.

Cook's encounter with the Fijians was a significant moment in Fiji's history, as it brought the islands to the attention of European powers and marked the beginning of European interest in the region. Cook's detailed accounts of his journey and his favorable descriptions of Fiji's beauty piqued the curiosity of other explorers and traders.

The 19th century saw an influx of European traders, missionaries, and adventurers to Fiji. These early European visitors brought with them a mix of curiosity, ambition, and the desire to exploit the islands' resources and establish influence in the region.

Christian missionaries, primarily from Britain, began arriving in Fiji in the early 19th century, aiming to spread Christianity and convert the local population. While their intentions were rooted in faith, their presence also played a role in the cultural and social transformations that lay ahead.

The pursuit of economic gains led European traders to Fiji's shores. The lucrative sandalwood trade attracted merchants from various European nations, such as the British and the French, who engaged in business dealings with the local Fijians. This trade, however, also introduced new dynamics and tensions among the indigenous communities.

By the mid-19th century, Fiji became entangled in the dark era of "blackbirding." This practice involved the recruitment and forced labor of thousands of laborers, mostly from India and other Pacific islands, to work on sugarcane plantations. The exploitation of indentured laborers not only brought about harsh living conditions but also had a lasting impact on the demographic makeup of Fiji, as it contributed to the growth of the Indo-Fijian community.

As European influence increased, so did the political complexities. In 1871, Fiji was ceded to Britain, and by 1874, it officially became a British Crown colony. This marked a turning point in Fiji's history as it came under British colonial rule, which lasted for nearly a century.

During the colonial era, British governors were appointed to govern Fiji, and their influence extended to various aspects of Fijian life, including land ownership and governance systems. The establishment of a colonial administration brought about significant changes to the social and political structures of the islands.

The British colonial period also witnessed the growth of the sugar industry. Large-scale sugarcane plantations were developed, primarily worked by indentured laborers from India. The sugar industry became a major economic driver for Fiji, shaping its economy and demographics.

Throughout the colonial era, Fijian chiefs retained some authority over their communities, and the British administration worked to navigate the delicate balance between colonial control and respecting indigenous customs and traditions.

In 1970, after nearly a century of British colonial rule, Fiji gained independence. Ratu Sir Kamisese Mara became the first Prime Minister of the newly independent nation, and Fiji embarked on a journey of nation-building and self-governance.

The arrival of Europeans and the subsequent colonial era forever transformed Fiji's landscape, society, and cultural identity. The interactions between European explorers, traders, missionaries, and the indigenous Fijians laid the groundwork for the complex and diverse nation we know today.

Struggles for Independence: Fiji's Path to Sovereignty

The struggles for independence mark a defining chapter in Fiji's history, as the nation navigated its way through political upheavals, challenges, and transformations on the path to sovereignty. The mid-20th century saw Fiji assert its desire for self-governance, shaping the destiny of its people and the future of the nation.

In the years leading up to World War II, Fiji experienced significant changes, including shifts in its political landscape and an emerging sense of nationalism. The demand for political representation and a voice in decision-making intensified, as the Fijian people sought to assert their right to self-determination.

During the war, Fiji played a vital role in the Pacific theater, contributing troops to the British and Allied forces. This participation in the war effort heightened the sense of national pride and fostered a growing belief that the Fijian people were capable of charting their own destiny.

The post-war era witnessed a surge in political activism and demands for greater autonomy. Political parties representing various communities and interests emerged, and debates over the future governance of Fiji intensified.

In 1965, Fiji took a significant step towards independence when the British colonial administration granted the nation self-governing status. The establishment of the Legislative Council allowed for a degree of local decision-making and marked a turning point in Fiji's journey towards self-determination.

However, the road to independence was not without challenges. The complexities of Fiji's multicultural society, with a diverse mix of indigenous Fijians, Indo-Fijians, and other ethnic groups, posed unique hurdles in the nation-building process. The delicate balance of power-sharing and ensuring the rights and representation of all communities became central to the discussions surrounding independence.

In 1970, Fiji finally achieved its long-awaited goal of independence from British colonial rule. On October 10th, 1970, the British Union Jack was lowered, and the Fijian flag was raised, symbolizing the birth of a new nation. Ratu Sir Kamisese Mara, a key figure in the nation's politics, became Fiji's first Prime Minister.

The independence celebrations marked a significant moment of unity and hope for the future, as Fijians of all backgrounds came together to celebrate their newfound sovereignty. The Fijian people demonstrated resilience and determination in overcoming the challenges they faced, forging a path towards a united and diverse nation.

In the years following independence, Fiji's political landscape continued to evolve. The multi-ethnic composition of the nation necessitated delicate negotiations to ensure that all communities had a stake in the governance of the country.

However, the journey towards stability was not without difficulties. In 1987, Fiji experienced its first coup d'état, driven by ethnic tensions and concerns over political representation. The events of 1987 sent shockwaves through the nation, raising questions about democracy, governance, and the inclusivity of the political system.

Subsequent coups in 2000 further tested Fiji's resolve and brought forth debates about the nation's future direction. The coup in 2000 resulted in an interim government and led to a period of political uncertainty.

Throughout these challenging times, the Fijian people demonstrated their commitment to preserving democracy and upholding the values of unity and inclusivity. The establishment of a multi-racial and multicultural society became a cornerstone of Fiji's identity and a testament to the nation's aspiration for a shared future.

In 2013, Fiji adopted a new constitution that aimed to foster a sense of national unity while recognizing the equal status of all citizens, irrespective of ethnicity. The constitution enshrined principles of inclusivity, non-discrimination, and equal opportunities for all.

Today, Fiji stands as a sovereign nation, celebrating its multicultural heritage and diversity while continuing to navigate the complexities of governance and nation-building. The struggles for independence have left an indelible mark on the national consciousness, reminding the Fijian people of the importance of unity and the pursuit of a shared vision for the future.

Modern Fiji: Society, Politics, and Economy

In the wake of its struggles for independence, Fiji entered the modern era with a newfound sense of identity and a vision for the future. Today, the nation stands as a thriving multicultural society, navigating its way through the complexities of politics and the challenges of building a robust economy.

Modern Fiji is a vibrant melting pot of cultures, with its population comprising various ethnicities, including indigenous Fijians, Indo-Fijians, Europeans, Chinese, and others. This diverse composition has shaped the nation's social fabric, where different communities coexist, celebrating their traditions while embracing a shared national identity.

The government of Fiji operates as a parliamentary democracy, with a President serving as the Head of State and a Prime Minister as the Head of Government. The Parliament, known as the Fijian Parliament, is the legislative body responsible for enacting laws and making decisions on behalf of the nation.

In the quest for political stability, Fiji has experienced periods of both democratic governance and military intervention. The coups of 1987 and 2000 brought moments of uncertainty, leading to periods of interim governance. However, the nation's commitment to democracy and national unity remains steadfast.

The 2013 constitution marked a significant step towards reinforcing the principles of inclusivity and equal representation. It abolished communal electoral rolls, which were based on ethnicity, and introduced a common roll, allowing all citizens to vote on equal terms. This move aimed to foster a sense of national unity and promote a more inclusive political landscape.

The economy of modern Fiji is diverse and multi-faceted. Key industries include tourism, agriculture, manufacturing, and services. Tourism plays a vital role in the nation's economic growth, drawing visitors from around the world to experience Fiji's stunning landscapes, warm hospitality, and vibrant culture. The pristine beaches, coral reefs, and luxurious resorts make Fiji a sought-after destination for travelers seeking a tropical paradise.

Agriculture also contributes significantly to Fiji's economy, with sugarcane being a prominent crop. Other agricultural products include root crops, coconuts, and tropical fruits. The fishing industry harnesses the abundance of marine resources surrounding the islands, providing sustenance and economic opportunities for coastal communities.

The manufacturing sector in Fiji includes food and beverage processing, textiles, and garment manufacturing. The nation's strategic location in the Pacific has facilitated trade and commerce, and Fiji has developed as a regional hub for financial services and offshore banking.

The Fijian government is dedicated to promoting sustainable development and addressing environmental challenges. Climate change poses significant threats to the island nation, including rising sea levels and extreme weather events. Fiji has taken a proactive stance on the global stage, advocating for climate action and sustainable practices.

In recent years, Fiji has made strides in addressing social issues and promoting gender equality. Efforts to enhance access to education and healthcare, along with initiatives to support women's empowerment and youth development, have been integral to the nation's progress.

Sports, particularly rugby, holds a special place in Fijian society. The Fijian rugby sevens team has achieved international acclaim, winning multiple World Rugby Sevens Series titles and Olympic gold medals. The passion for sports reflects the nation's camaraderie and determination to excel on the world stage.

Modern Fiji continues to embrace its rich cultural heritage, with traditional practices, arts, and crafts interwoven into everyday life. Fijians take pride in their unique cultural expressions, from dance and music to storytelling and ceremonies.

As Fiji strides forward into the 21st century, the nation faces a balancing act of preserving its cultural identity, protecting its environment, and steering its economy towards sustainable growth. The spirit of resilience and unity that defined its struggles for independence remains a guiding force as Fiji shapes its destiny on the world stage.

The Geographical Diversity of Fiji

Nestled in the heart of the South Pacific Ocean, Fiji is a land of breathtaking geographical diversity. The archipelago is made up of over 300 islands, each offering a unique and captivating landscape for visitors to explore.

The islands of Fiji can be categorized into two main groups: the larger islands, including Viti Levu and Vanua Levu, and the smaller islands, which form the outer regions. Viti Levu, the largest of them all, serves as the hub of economic and political activities, with the capital city, Suva, situated on its southeastern coast.

The geographical wonders of Fiji are vast and varied. From lush rainforests and soaring mountain ranges to pristine beaches and vibrant coral reefs, Fiji boasts an array of natural treasures that leave travelers spellbound.

The interior of Viti Levu is dominated by rugged terrain, with majestic peaks and fertile valleys. Mount Tomanivi, also known as Mount Victoria, stands tall as Fiji's highest point, offering a challenging but rewarding hiking experience to those seeking a panoramic view of the surrounding landscape.

As we venture towards the coastlines, we are greeted by picturesque beaches adorned with swaying coconut palms and turquoise waters. The Coral Coast, located on the southern shores of Viti Levu, is a popular destination for its stunning coral reefs and world-class diving and snorkeling opportunities.

The Yasawa and Mamanuca Islands, lying off the western coast of Viti Levu, showcase Fiji's renowned paradise-like beauty. These smaller islands boast white sandy beaches, crystal-clear lagoons, and luxurious resorts, making them a sought-after destination for relaxation and romance.

Heading northward, we find the island of Vanua Levu, Fiji's second-largest island. Here, a different kind of allure awaits with dense rainforests, cascading waterfalls, and hidden gems like the picturesque Savusavu Bay.

Beyond Viti Levu and Vanua Levu, Fiji's smaller islands are gems waiting to be explored. Taveuni, often referred to as the "Garden

Island," is renowned for its lush vegetation, abundant wildlife, and natural wonders like the Bouma National Heritage Park.

The Lau Group, located in the eastern reaches of Fiji, is an archipelago composed of 57 islands, each boasting its own unique character. These remote islands offer an escape into untouched beauty, where traditional Fijian customs and natural splendor converge.

Fiji's geographical diversity extends to its inland waterways. Rivers and waterfalls meander through the landscape, providing opportunities for river safaris and thrilling adventures like whitewater rafting.

The underwater world of Fiji is equally captivating. The nation's coral reefs are teeming with marine life, making it a paradise for snorkelers and divers alike. Rainbow-colored fish, graceful manta rays, and the majestic humpback whales are just a few of the wonders awaiting beneath the waves.

The geography of Fiji is not just limited to its land and sea. The islands are dotted with hot springs and mud pools, where visitors can indulge in natural spa experiences. The Sabeto Hot Springs and Mud Pool, near Nadi, are renowned for their healing properties and offer a rejuvenating escape.

The geographical diversity of Fiji isn't just a feast for the eyes—it also plays a crucial role in the nation's ecosystem and biodiversity. The rainforests are home to an array of endemic plant and animal species, while the coastlines support diverse marine life.

The People of Fiji: Diversity and Traditions

The people of Fiji are as diverse as the geographical landscape that surrounds them. Rooted in ancient heritage and shaped by centuries of cultural interactions, the Fijian population reflects a tapestry of traditions, languages, and customs that contribute to the vibrant and harmonious society we witness today.

At the heart of Fijian culture are the indigenous Fijians, also known as iTaukei, who trace their ancestry back to the earliest settlers of the islands. With a deep connection to the land and the ocean, the iTaukei people continue to embrace traditional customs and practices that have been passed down through generations.

The iTaukei are renowned for their hospitality, warmth, and a strong sense of community. Village life remains an integral part of their identity, where communal living and respect for elders are cherished values. Traditional ceremonies, such as the Yaqona (Kava) ceremony, symbolize the spirit of friendship and welcome that is extended to visitors.

A significant part of Fijian culture is the Meke, a form of storytelling through song and dance. The Meke showcases historical events, legends, and myths, preserving the nation's oral traditions and celebrating its rich heritage. These captivating performances are a reflection of the Fijian people's pride in their cultural identity.

As we explore the diversity of Fiji, we encounter the Indo-Fijian community, whose roots can be traced back to the 19th-century "blackbirding" era when thousands of laborers were brought to the islands to work on sugarcane plantations. The Indo-Fijians have preserved their cultural heritage, language, and religious traditions, adding a unique and colorful dimension to Fiji's multicultural fabric.

The Hindu and Muslim festivals of Diwali and Eid are celebrated with great enthusiasm, showcasing the vibrant cultural expressions of the Indo-Fijian community. These festivals are occasions for feasting, social gatherings, and expressions of gratitude and devotion.

The Chinese community in Fiji is another integral part of the nation's diverse identity. Many Chinese families migrated to Fiji during the 19th and early 20th centuries, seeking new opportunities in commerce and trade. Their contributions to the nation's economic and cultural landscape are evident, with Chinese traditions and festivals being celebrated throughout the country.

The influence of other ethnic communities, such as Europeans and Pacific Islanders, adds to the rich tapestry of Fiji's multicultural society. The blend of cultures is evident in the nation's cuisine, with dishes featuring flavors from around the world, making the Fijian dining experience a delightful fusion of tastes and textures.

Language plays a significant role in shaping cultural identity, and Fiji boasts three official languages: Fijian, English, and Hindi. The Fijian language, which belongs to the Austronesian language family, is the mother tongue of the iTaukei community, with various dialects spoken across the islands. English serves as the language of administration and education, while Hindi is spoken by the Indo-Fijian community.

Religious diversity is also a defining feature of Fijian society. The majority of iTaukei practice Christianity, with various denominations represented. Hinduism and Islam are practiced by the Indo-Fijian community, and there is a smaller percentage of Buddhists, Sikhs, and other faiths, showcasing the nation's acceptance and respect for religious freedom.

As we immerse ourselves in the traditions and diversity of the Fijian people, we witness a society that cherishes its roots while embracing the world's cultural tapestry. The spirit of unity and respect for one another's traditions is at the core of Fijian identity, fostering a sense of harmony and celebration of diversity.

Cultural Melting Pot: Influences and Traditions

In the heart of the South Pacific, Fiji stands as a living testament to the beauty of cultural diversity and the power of harmonious coexistence. The nation's history as a crossroads of cultures has shaped a unique cultural melting pot, where influences from various communities have interwoven to create a rich and vibrant tapestry of traditions.

As we delve into the cultural landscape of Fiji, we encounter the indigenous Fijians, the iTaukei, whose ancient traditions are deeply rooted in the land and sea. The Meke, a captivating display of storytelling through song and dance, showcases the resilience of Fijian oral traditions and their reverence for history and myths.

The iTaukei's traditional art of wood carving, known as "masi," has been passed down through generations, producing intricate designs on tapa cloth. The motifs and patterns found in masi are a visual expression of the Fijian people's connection to their natural surroundings and ancestral spirits.

Fijian cuisine is a fusion of flavors and influences from various communities. Lovo, a traditional feast cooked in an underground earth oven, highlights the iTaukei's culinary heritage, with foods such as taro, yams, and fish being staples. The infusion of Indian spices and cooking techniques brought by the Indo-Fijians adds an array of aromatic curries, chutneys, and sweet treats to the culinary repertoire.

The Hindu festival of Diwali, the "Festival of Lights," is celebrated with fervor by the Indo-Fijian community, illuminating the night skies with oil lamps and fireworks. This joyous occasion signifies the triumph of light over darkness and serves as a reminder of the unity that transcends cultural boundaries.

The vibrant colors and energetic rhythms of Bollywood dance are a testament to the Indo-Fijian community's celebration of their heritage. The graceful movements and expressive performances of this dance form are a reflection of the community's love for art and storytelling.

The Chinese influence in Fiji is evident in the celebration of Chinese New Year, where the streets come alive with lion and dragon dances, and red lanterns adorn the cityscape. The Chinese community's dedication to preserving their heritage is reflected in their continued practice of traditional customs and ancestral worship.

The diverse religious landscape of Fiji fosters an environment of respect and tolerance. Places of worship, including churches, temples, mosques, and gurdwaras, stand side by side, a testament to the nation's commitment to religious freedom and understanding.

Fiji's annual Hibiscus Festival is a vibrant celebration of the nation's multicultural identity. The festival brings together various communities to showcase their talents, cuisine, and cultural expressions, fostering a sense of unity and mutual appreciation.

The music of Fiji reflects the blending of cultures, with traditional Fijian tunes blending with Indian, Polynesian, and Western influences. From the melodious harmonies of the "meke" to the lively rhythms of Indian "bhajans," music serves as a bridge that connects communities and uplifts spirits.

Fijians embrace traditional ceremonies and rituals while embracing modernity. Weddings, funerals, and rites of passage are occasions for communities to come together, reaffirming the bonds that unite them.

The Fijian way of life embraces a spirit of togetherness, known as "vei lomani," which means "love one another." This ethos permeates the nation's social fabric and is a driving force in building a harmonious and inclusive society.

Fijian Art and Craftsmanship

Fijian art and craftsmanship are a reflection of the nation's rich cultural heritage and the creative ingenuity of its people. For centuries, the Fijians have expressed their stories, beliefs, and way of life through a myriad of artistic forms, showcasing their mastery in various art forms and craftsmanship.

One of the most iconic art forms in Fiji is wood carving, known as "masi." Fijian craftsmen intricately carve designs onto tapa cloth, using traditional tools passed down through generations. The motifs on masi often depict symbols of nature, ancestral spirits, and important historical events, making each piece a unique and symbolic representation of Fijian identity.

The art of masi holds immense cultural significance. It is used in ceremonies, such as weddings and funerals, as well as in storytelling performances like the Meke. The Meke is a captivating display of song and dance that brings to life the stories of Fijian history and myths, and masi often adorns the performers' costumes, amplifying the visual storytelling.

Another notable form of Fijian art is pottery. Fijian potters skillfully create exquisite clay vessels and containers using traditional techniques. The art of pottery has a practical purpose, with pottery items being used in everyday life, such as for cooking, storage, and ceremonies.

The design of pottery is also influenced by Fijian culture, featuring intricate patterns and symbols that hold cultural significance. Each pottery item is not just a functional object but also a work of art that embodies the creative spirit of the Fijian people.

Fijian handicrafts extend beyond masi and pottery to include a wide range of artistic expressions. The making of woven mats, baskets, and traditional crafts using natural materials like pandanus leaves and coconut fibers is a cherished tradition.

These handicrafts are not only functional but also serve as valuable cultural artifacts. The intricate weaving patterns and craftsmanship are passed down through families, preserving the knowledge and techniques of these traditional arts.

The people of Fiji have also excelled in the art of storytelling through visual representation. Traditional Fijian tattoos, known as "tatau" or "tatu," are a form of body art that holds spiritual and cultural significance. The tattoos are intricately designed and were historically used to indicate social status, achievements, and affiliations within the community.

Today, tattoo artists in Fiji draw inspiration from traditional Fijian motifs and patterns to create modern tattoo designs that honor the past while embracing contemporary aesthetics.

Fijian culture also celebrates the art of dance and music. The energetic and rhythmic dances, such as the "meke," showcase the grace and skill of Fijian performers. Music, including traditional songs and instruments like the lali drum and guitar, are essential elements of Fijian celebrations and gatherings, uniting communities through the power of rhythm and melody.

As Fiji continues to evolve and embrace modernity, traditional arts and craftsmanship persist as an integral part of the nation's cultural identity. The Fijian people take immense pride in their artistic heritage, ensuring that these timeless traditions are preserved and passed down to future generations.

Celebrating Life: Festivals and Ceremonies

In the enchanting islands of Fiji, life is a vibrant celebration of culture, traditions, and joyous occasions. Festivals and ceremonies hold a special place in the hearts of the Fijian people, providing a glimpse into the nation's rich heritage and the spirit of unity that binds its communities.

The Fijian calendar is brimming with festivities that honor religious, cultural, and historical significance. One of the most celebrated festivals is Diwali, the Hindu "Festival of Lights." Diwali is a time of illumination and joy, with homes adorned with colorful lights, oil lamps, and intricate rangoli designs. Families come together to share delicious sweets, exchange gifts, and offer prayers to seek blessings from the deities.

The celebration of Eid, the Muslim festival that marks the end of Ramadan, is another cherished occasion in Fiji. Muslims gather for prayers and thanksgiving, followed by communal feasting and sharing of meals with family and friends.

The Hibiscus Festival, an annual extravaganza, is a symbol of Fiji's multicultural unity. The festival showcases various communities, with participants donning traditional attire and showcasing their talents in dance, music, and crafts. It is a grand celebration of diversity and a reflection of the Fijian spirit of togetherness.

The Bula Festival in Nadi is a vibrant week-long event that features beauty pageants, talent shows, and cultural performances. The festival celebrates Fijian culture and promotes tourism, drawing visitors from around the world to experience the essence of Fiji's hospitality and traditions.

The Fiji Day celebration on October 10th marks the nation's independence from British colonial rule. The day is commemorated with parades, flag-raising ceremonies, and cultural performances that display the pride and unity of the Fijian people.

Fijians hold traditional ceremonies with deep reverence for their heritage and ancestors. The Yaqona (Kava) ceremony, in which kava, a traditional drink, is consumed, is an integral part of Fijian life. The ceremony fosters a sense of community, with participants bonding over the ritual and sharing of kava, which is believed to have calming and unifying properties.

Weddings and funerals are significant milestones in Fijian life and are marked with traditional ceremonies. Weddings are joyous occasions filled with colorful attire, dance, and music, while funerals are solemn events where communities come together to mourn and pay their respects to the departed.

The Lovo feast is a traditional Fijian celebration of food and togetherness. Food is prepared by cooking it in an underground earth oven, which infuses the dishes with smoky flavors and tender textures. The Lovo feast is a time for families and communities to share in the bounty of the land and the sea, fostering a sense of unity and gratitude.

The Fijian Way of Life: Customs and Etiquette

In the heart of the South Pacific, Fiji beckons with its warm hospitality and a way of life that embraces a spirit of togetherness. The Fijian people take immense pride in their customs and etiquette, which play a central role in defining their cultural identity and fostering strong bonds within the community.

One of the key elements of Fijian culture is respect for elders and authority figures. The Fijian society places great importance on showing deference and courtesy to those who hold positions of authority or are older in age. This respect is demonstrated through gestures like bowing the head slightly or using formal titles when addressing elders.

The concept of "vei lomani," which translates to "love one another," is at the core of the Fijian way of life. This ethos encourages people to treat one another with kindness, compassion, and empathy. It forms the basis for the tight-knit community bonds that are characteristic of Fijian society.

The Fijian people are known for their warm smiles and welcoming demeanor. When meeting someone for the first time, it is customary to exchange "Bula!" - the Fijian word for hello - with a bright smile, establishing an instant connection.

Hospitality is deeply ingrained in Fijian culture. Visitors are welcomed with open arms and treated as honored guests. The offering of Yaqona (Kava) to visitors is a common ritual, symbolizing friendship and goodwill. Accepting the Yaqona is considered a sign of respect for the host.

The art of gift-giving is an integral part of Fijian customs. When visiting someone's home or attending a celebration, it is customary to bring a small gift, such as fruit, sweets, or a handicraft, as a token of appreciation and respect.

Fijians cherish their traditional ceremonies, and it is essential to show reverence and observe the appropriate etiquette during these occasions. Dressing modestly and showing humility are expected during ceremonies, especially when participating in sacred rituals.

When entering a Fijian village, visitors are encouraged to seek permission from the village chief or an elder. This act of seeking permission, known as "sevusevu," is a mark of respect and acknowledgement of the village's authority.

Language plays a significant role in Fijian etiquette. Learning a few basic phrases in the Fijian language, such as "vinaka" (thank you) and "sota tale" (goodbye), goes a long way in showing respect and appreciation for the local culture.

Fijians value punctuality, particularly when attending events or gatherings. Arriving on time is seen as a sign of respect for the host and the other attendees.

In Fijian culture, personal space is less defined, and physical contact is common during interactions. Handshakes, hugs, and shoulder pats are used to convey warmth and affection, even among acquaintances.

While Fijians are generally warm and friendly, it is essential to be sensitive to cultural norms and customs. Avoiding sensitive topics, such as politics and religion, in casual conversations is advisable, as these subjects can be divisive.

The traditional Fijian dress, known as "sulu," is often worn on formal occasions and celebrations. Visitors are encouraged to embrace local customs by wearing appropriate attire, such as sulu or modest clothing, when attending ceremonies or entering places of worship.

Respecting the environment and the natural world is a fundamental aspect of the Fijian way of life. The Fijian people have a deep connection to their land and ocean, and they take great care to preserve and protect their natural resources for future generations.

Religions in Fiji: Spirituality and Beliefs

In the picturesque islands of Fiji, spirituality weaves a diverse tapestry of beliefs and faiths that reflect the nation's multicultural identity. The people of Fiji embrace a range of religions, each contributing to the rich cultural landscape and fostering a spirit of unity and tolerance.

One of the predominant religions in Fiji is Christianity, which was introduced by European missionaries during the 19th century. The majority of indigenous Fijians, the iTaukei, practice Christianity, with various denominations, including Methodism, Catholicism, and Anglicanism, being prevalent. Churches play a central role in Fijian communities, serving as places of worship, social gatherings, and spiritual guidance.

The Indo-Fijian community brought Hinduism to Fiji during the period of indentured labor in the late 19th and early 20th centuries. Hindu temples, or mandirs, are widespread across the islands, and festivals such as Diwali and Holi are celebrated with great enthusiasm. The vibrant colors, decorative rangoli patterns, and traditional music create an atmosphere of joy and devotion during these occasions.

Islam also holds a significant presence in Fiji, practiced predominantly by the Indo-Fijian community. Mosques serve as places of worship and centers of Islamic education, and the holy month of Ramadan is observed with fasting, prayer, and community gatherings. Eid ul-Fitr, marking the end of Ramadan, is a joyous occasion for Muslims in Fiji to come together in celebration and gratitude.

The Chinese community in Fiji has preserved their traditional beliefs, such as Buddhism, Taoism, and Confucianism. Temples and shrines dedicated to these faiths can be found in cities and towns across the islands. The Chinese New Year is a time of colorful celebrations, with lion and dragon dances, firecrackers, and offerings to ancestors for blessings and prosperity in the coming year.

Fiji's religious diversity is not limited to these major faiths alone. Other religious communities, including Sikhs, Baha'is, and various smaller denominations, contribute to the nation's religious fabric. The Fijian government upholds the principle of religious freedom, ensuring that people of all faiths have the right to practice their beliefs without discrimination.

Despite the diversity of beliefs, Fiji's religious communities coexist harmoniously, promoting interfaith dialogue and understanding. The nation is a shining example of unity in diversity, where people from different religious backgrounds come together to celebrate festivals, share in each other's joys, and support one another in times of need.

Fijians also retain a deep connection to their ancestral spirits and traditional beliefs. The concept of mana, the spiritual power that exists in all living things, is integral to Fijian spirituality. Traditional ceremonies and rituals are performed to seek guidance from ancestral spirits and to maintain harmony with the natural world.

Fijian Cuisine: A Gastronomic Journey

Embarking on a gastronomic journey through the enchanting islands of Fiji is a delightful experience that tantalizes the taste buds and leaves a lasting impression on every traveler's palate. Fijian cuisine is a fusion of flavors, influenced by the nation's diverse cultural heritage and the abundance of fresh ingredients sourced from both land and sea.

At the heart of Fijian cuisine is a deep appreciation for the bountiful gifts of nature. The fertile land produces a variety of root crops, such as taro, cassava, and yams, which form the foundation of many traditional dishes. These starchy staples are rich in nutrients and are often accompanied by delectable side dishes and sauces.

The traditional Fijian Lovo feast is a culinary spectacle that showcases the art of cooking with natural elements. The feast involves the preparation of a variety of foods, including meats, fish, and vegetables, wrapped in banana leaves and cooked in an underground earth oven. The result is a harmonious blend of smoky flavors and tender textures that elevate the dining experience to a new level.

Seafood holds a special place in Fijian cuisine, given the nation's proximity to the ocean. Fresh fish, such as mahi-mahi, tuna, and snapper, are staples in coastal communities. Kokoda, a Fijian ceviche, is a popular dish that features raw fish marinated in coconut cream and citrus juices, creating a refreshing and zesty flavor profile.

Coconuts are a ubiquitous ingredient in Fijian cooking. Coconut milk and grated coconut are used to add richness and depth to curries, stews, and desserts. The coconut palm, often referred to as the "tree of life," provides not only culinary delights but also materials for handicrafts, shelter, and traditional ceremonies.

The blending of cultures in Fiji has given rise to a delectable array of dishes that draw inspiration from different culinary traditions. Indian influence is evident in the vibrant curries, chutneys, and spices that add a burst of aromatic flavors to Fijian cuisine. Roti, an Indian flatbread, is a favorite accompaniment to many dishes.

The Fijian love for spices and herbs is evident in the use of turmeric, ginger, garlic, and chili peppers, which infuse dishes with layers of complexity. The fusion of these bold flavors with fresh, locally sourced produce is a hallmark of Fijian cooking.

The Yaqona, also known as Kava, is a traditional drink that holds cultural significance in Fijian society. Made from the root of the Piper methysticum plant, Yaqona is consumed during ceremonial occasions and social gatherings. The drink has calming properties and fosters a sense of community and camaraderie among those partaking in the ritual.

Fijian desserts are a delightful conclusion to any meal. Tropical fruits, such as papaya, pineapple, and mango, are often served fresh or in delectable desserts like fruit salads and pies. Lolo buns, coconut buns filled with jam or caramel, are a favorite treat enjoyed by locals and visitors alike.

Exotic Delights: Exploring Fijian Dishes

Prepare to embark on a culinary adventure like no other as we explore the exotic delights of Fijian dishes. The vibrant and diverse cuisine of Fiji reflects the nation's cultural melting pot, infusing flavors from various communities and celebrating the abundance of natural resources found across the islands.

Let's start our journey with the iconic Fijian Lovo feast. This traditional cooking method involves preparing an assortment of meats, fish, and vegetables, which are then wrapped in banana leaves and cooked in an underground earth oven. The slow cooking process infuses the ingredients with smoky flavors, creating tender and succulent dishes that capture the essence of Fiji's rich culinary heritage.

One of the stars of Fijian cuisine is Kokoda, a refreshing and tangy ceviche made with raw fish marinated in coconut cream and citrus juices. The zesty flavors of lime and lemon complement the sweetness of the coconut cream, resulting in a delightful balance that awakens the taste buds.

Dive into the ocean's bounty with Fijian seafood dishes. Freshly caught fish, such as mahi-mahi, tuna, and snapper, are expertly prepared and served in a variety of mouthwatering ways. Grilled fish with a sprinkle of local spices, baked fish with coconut milk, and fish curry are just a few examples of the seafood delights that await.

Taro, a root crop widely cultivated in Fiji, takes center stage in many traditional dishes. Taro leaves are used to wrap and cook meat and seafood, infusing the dish with a distinctive earthy flavor. Dalo (taro root) is also boiled, mashed, and served with coconut cream to create a comforting and hearty side dish.

Indulge in the aromatic and bold flavors of Fijian curries. Influenced by Indian cuisine, Fijian curries boast a tantalizing blend of spices, such as turmeric, cumin, coriander, and mustard seeds. Chicken, lamb, or seafood are often used as the protein base, making each curry a delightful explosion of taste.

Bread lovers will delight in Fijian roti, a soft and flaky flatbread that perfectly complements curries or can be enjoyed on its own.

Whether stuffed with savory fillings or topped with sweet condiments, roti is a versatile and beloved staple in Fijian dining.

For those with a sweet tooth, Fijian desserts offer a delightful treat. Fresh tropical fruits like papaya, pineapple, and mango are served as refreshing and juicy delights. If you're craving something more decadent, try the lolo buns - coconut buns filled with jam or caramel - a delightful and indulgent treat.

The Yaqona ceremony, also known as the Kava ceremony, is an integral part of Fijian culture and social gatherings. Yaqona, made from the root of the Piper methysticum plant, is a traditional drink with calming properties. It fosters a sense of community and camaraderie as participants come together to share in the ritual and the drink.

From Sea to Plate: The Bounty of Fiji's Waters

When it comes to the culinary delights of Fiji, the bountiful waters that surround the islands play a starring role. The ocean is a cornucopia of treasures, offering a diverse array of seafood that graces the plates of Fijians and delights the palates of visitors from around the world.

Fiji's pristine marine environment teems with an abundant variety of fish, making it a paradise for seafood enthusiasts. Mahi-mahi, with its firm and flaky flesh, is a favorite catch, often served grilled or pan-seared to preserve its natural flavors. Tuna, another prized fish, is served as sashimi, grilled steaks, or even in a traditional Fijian kokoda, where the fish is marinated in a tangy blend of coconut cream and citrus juices.

Snapper, known for its mild and sweet taste, is a versatile fish that can be prepared in numerous ways, from being baked with local herbs to being pan-fried with a dash of island spices. Barramundi, a fish native to the Pacific region, is a delicacy loved for its delicate texture and delicate flavor, often served with a squeeze of fresh lime for a delightful zing.

But the ocean's bounty extends beyond fish. Fijian waters are home to an array of shellfish and crustaceans that grace the plates of seafood aficionados. Lobster, with its succulent and tender meat, is a luxurious treat, often prepared grilled or in a rich buttery sauce. Crab, whether it's mud crab or blue swimmer crab, is prized for its sweet and delicate flavor, making it a popular choice for seafood lovers.

Prawns, whether they are jumbo tiger prawns or freshwater river prawns, are cooked in a myriad of ways - from being stir-fried with garlic and chili to being served in a creamy coconut curry. These crustaceans add a burst of flavor and texture to Fijian seafood dishes, elevating them to gourmet status.

The seas around Fiji also harbor a variety of shellfish, such as clams and mussels. These delectable mollusks are often featured in seafood soups and stews, creating hearty and comforting dishes that are perfect for cool evenings by the beach.

And let's not forget about the cephalopods that grace Fijian waters. Squid and octopus find their way into many traditional dishes, adding a unique and chewy texture to the culinary landscape. They are often marinated, grilled, or included in seafood salads, showcasing the versatility of Fijian seafood cuisine.

The bounty of Fiji's waters isn't limited to fish and shellfish alone. Seaweed and sea grapes, known as "kare" and "kai," respectively, are commonly used in Fijian cuisine. These nutritious marine plants add a touch of umami flavor to dishes and are often enjoyed in salads or as side accompaniments to seafood delicacies.

Fijians' reverence for their marine environment extends to sustainable fishing practices. Traditional fishing methods, such as handline fishing and spearfishing, are still practiced, ensuring that the ocean's resources are conserved for future generations.

As we savor the delights from sea to plate, we discover a culinary journey that celebrates the ocean's gifts and the Fijian people's deep connection to their marine environment. The bounty of Fiji's waters is a testament to the nation's commitment to preserving its natural resources and sustaining the vibrant seafood culture that is an integral part of Fijian identity.

Wildlife of Fiji: Exploring Flora and Fauna

As we delve into the heart of Fiji's wilderness, we uncover a fascinating tapestry of flora and fauna that thrives in the lush landscapes and crystal-clear waters of the islands. Fiji's unique location in the South Pacific fosters a diverse ecosystem, where tropical rainforests, vibrant coral reefs, and abundant marine life coexist harmoniously.

Let's begin our journey by exploring Fiji's enchanting flora. The islands are adorned with a stunning array of plant species, many of which are endemic and found nowhere else on Earth. Lush tropical rainforests are home to towering mahogany trees, ancient banyans, and majestic ferns that create a verdant canopy overhead. The scent of exotic blooms, such as hibiscus, frangipani, and orchids, fills the air, adding a touch of paradise to Fiji's landscape.

One of Fiji's unique plants is the "Tagimoucia" flower, known as the "Flower of Love." Found on the slopes of the extinct volcano Mount Tomanivi, this striking crimson and white flower holds cultural significance in Fijian folklore, symbolizing eternal love and devotion.

Venturing underwater, Fiji's marine life is equally captivating. The surrounding seas are a haven for diverse marine species, making it a paradise for snorkelers and divers. The coral reefs teem with colorful fish, such as parrotfish, angelfish, and clownfish, while manta rays gracefully glide through the crystal-clear waters.

Fiji is renowned for its shark populations, and shark conservation efforts have been instrumental in protecting these majestic creatures. Divers have the rare opportunity to encounter various shark species, including the impressive bull sharks and the awe-inspiring tiger sharks.

The vibrant sea fans, delicate sea anemones, and towering coral formations create a kaleidoscope of colors beneath the waves. These coral reefs are not only a breathtaking sight but also serve as crucial habitats for a myriad of marine life.

Fiji's forests and coastal areas are home to a diverse range of wildlife. The islands are home to numerous bird species, such as the Fiji banded iguana and the vibrant orange dove. Birdwatchers will be delighted to spot the striking orange-breasted myzomela and the unique Kadavu fantail, both found exclusively in Fiji.

Fiji's rainforests provide sanctuary to various reptiles and amphibians, including the charming Pacific tree frog and the endemic Fiji banded snake. The island's ecosystems are delicate, and conservation efforts play a vital role in safeguarding the unique wildlife that calls Fiji home.

The Fijian waters are not only abundant in marine life but also boast impressive underwater caves and caverns. These hidden wonders offer divers the chance to explore mysterious and breathtaking subterranean landscapes.

Fiji's natural beauty extends to its national parks and protected areas. The Bouma National Heritage Park on Taveuni Island encompasses diverse ecosystems, from rainforests and waterfalls to coral reefs. The Sigatoka Sand Dunes National Park, on the other hand, showcases stunning sand dunes and unique plant species.

Marvels of the Ocean: Fiji's Marine Life

Beneath the azure waters that embrace the islands of Fiji lies a mesmerizing world of marine wonders. Fiji's marine life is an underwater paradise, where colorful coral reefs, majestic creatures, and a diverse array of fish create an awe-inspiring tapestry of life.

Fiji's coral reefs are some of the most diverse and vibrant in the world. Teeming with life, these underwater ecosystems are home to an astounding variety of coral species, including hard corals, soft corals, and sea fans. The intricate structures of the reefs provide shelter and feeding grounds for countless marine organisms.

Venturing into Fiji's crystal-clear waters, divers and snorkelers are greeted by a symphony of colors. Schools of tropical fish, such as parrotfish, butterflyfish, and angelfish, dart among the corals in a dazzling display of hues. Clownfish, with their striking orange and white patterns, peep out from the protective embrace of sea anemones.

Fiji's waters are a sanctuary for sea turtles, including the hawksbill, green, and loggerhead turtles. These graceful creatures gracefully glide through the waters, their movements a testament to the unspoiled environment that Fiji strives to protect.

Manta rays, with their impressive wingspans, elegantly soar through the currents, offering a breathtaking spectacle for lucky divers who encounter them. These gentle giants add to the allure of Fiji's underwater world, drawing in underwater photographers and nature enthusiasts from around the globe.

Sharks are another marvel of Fiji's marine life. The waters surrounding the islands are home to various shark species, including the impressive bull sharks and the majestic tiger sharks. Shark conservation efforts in Fiji have been instrumental in protecting these apex predators and promoting their importance in maintaining the balance of marine ecosystems.

Beyond the reefs, Fiji's underwater caves and caverns create a mysterious world waiting to be explored. Divers can venture into these subterranean wonders, discovering hidden chambers adorned with stalactites and stalagmites, and occasionally encountering elusive creatures that have made these caves their sanctuary.

The seasonal migration of marine life adds to the excitement of exploring Fiji's waters. From May to October, the majestic humpback whales grace the waters of Fiji as they embark on their annual journey. Witnessing these gentle giants breach and play in the open ocean is an unforgettable experience.

Fiji's commitment to marine conservation and sustainable tourism ensures that these marvels of the ocean will continue to flourish. Marine protected areas and conservation initiatives are in place to safeguard the delicate ecosystems and the magnificent creatures that call Fiji's waters home.

The marine life of Fiji is not only a source of wonder for visitors but also a source of livelihood for local communities. Sustainable fishing practices and eco-friendly tourism initiatives enable Fijians to coexist with nature, cherishing and protecting the treasures of the ocean.

Eco-Tourism in Fiji: Preserving Nature's Treasures

In the pristine islands of Fiji, a remarkable commitment to eco-tourism is woven into the fabric of the nation's identity. As travelers from around the world seek to immerse themselves in the enchanting beauty of Fiji's landscapes, the Fijian people hold steadfast to their responsibility as stewards of nature's treasures.

Eco-tourism in Fiji is more than just a trend; it is a way of life. The concept revolves around responsible travel that minimizes the impact on the environment while maximizing the benefits to local communities. Fiji's pristine natural wonders, from lush rainforests to vibrant coral reefs, are recognized as valuable assets that must be protected for future generations.

The Fijian government and local communities have established marine protected areas and national parks to safeguard the delicate ecosystems and preserve the biodiversity that thrives within them. These initiatives are designed not only to conserve marine life but also to offer travelers the opportunity to experience the wonders of nature without disrupting the delicate balance of the environment.

Eco-lodges and eco-resorts have sprung up across the islands, each designed to harmonize with the natural surroundings. These sustainable accommodations blend seamlessly into the landscapes, allowing guests to immerse themselves in the beauty of Fiji without leaving a significant ecological footprint.

In addition to promoting eco-friendly accommodations, Fiji's eco-tourism practices extend to the activities offered to visitors. Guided tours focus on education, with expert naturalists and guides providing insight into the local ecosystems and the efforts made to protect them. Travelers are encouraged to explore and appreciate the natural wonders while also learning about the delicate balance of life within these habitats.

Snorkeling and diving excursions adhere to strict guidelines to ensure the protection of coral reefs and marine life. Visitors are educated on responsible practices, such as maintaining a safe distance from marine creatures and refraining from touching or damaging coral formations. By empowering tourists with knowledge, Fiji fosters a sense of responsibility and respect for the marine environment.

Community-based tourism is a key component of eco-tourism in Fiji. Local villages welcome visitors, offering them the chance to experience authentic Fijian culture while contributing directly to the well-being of the community. Income from tourism helps support local schools, healthcare facilities, and infrastructure development, strengthening the ties between travelers and the people of Fiji.

Eco-tourism in Fiji also embraces sustainable agricultural practices. Organic farming and the use of traditional farming methods promote food security and reduce the reliance on imported goods. These practices not only support local communities but also contribute to the conservation of the islands' natural resources.

Fiji's commitment to eco-tourism has earned recognition and awards from various international organizations. The nation is a leading advocate for environmental conservation and sustainable tourism practices in the South Pacific region.

By embracing eco-tourism, Fiji has managed to strike a harmonious balance between nurturing nature's treasures and sharing them with the world. Travelers to Fiji have the privilege of experiencing a destination where pristine beauty and cultural heritage are cherished, protected, and shared with utmost care.

Top Natural Attractions: A Paradise for Adventurers

Welcome to the paradise of Fiji, where the natural wonders will leave you awe-inspired and beckon the adventurous at heart. The islands are a playground for explorers, offering a diverse array of top natural attractions that will captivate and exhilarate all who dare to venture into this tropical haven.

Let's begin our journey with the Sigatoka Sand Dunes, a testament to the eons of time that have shaped Fiji's landscape. These majestic dunes, located on the island of Viti Levu, tower up to 60 meters high and stretch along the coast for miles. A visit to the dunes promises stunning vistas of the ocean meeting the sand, creating a scene that seems like it's straight out of a dream.

Next on our list are the enchanting Bouma National Heritage Park and the Tavoro Waterfalls on Taveuni Island. The park is a tapestry of natural beauty, where tropical rainforests, lush flora, and native wildlife create an ecological wonderland. Hiking trails meander through the forests, leading to the Tavoro Waterfalls, where cascading waters plunge into pristine natural pools, inviting visitors to take a refreshing dip.

For the adventurous souls, Fiji's Kula Eco Park offers the chance to get up close and personal with the local flora and fauna. This sanctuary is dedicated to the preservation and conservation of Fiji's indigenous species, including the colorful Fiji banded iguana and the striking orange dove. The park serves as an educational hub, imparting knowledge about the delicate ecosystems that thrive within the islands.

If you're seeking an adrenaline rush, head to the Navua River for a thrilling whitewater rafting experience. The river flows through lush rainforests and cascades over thrilling rapids, providing an exhilarating journey through Fiji's untouched wilderness. Rafting down the Navua River is an adventure that combines adrenaline-pumping excitement with breathtaking natural beauty.

Fiji's underwater realm is a diver's paradise, and the Great Astrolabe Reef stands out as one of the world's largest barrier reefs. This majestic coral reef stretches over 100 kilometers, hosting an extraordinary diversity of marine life. Divers and snorkelers can encounter vibrant corals, colorful fish, and even the majestic manta rays that grace these waters.

The Yasawa Islands offer a plethora of natural delights for adventurers. From hiking trails that lead to panoramic vistas to hidden caves awaiting exploration, the Yasawas are a treasure trove of discoveries. Snorkeling in the coral gardens and swimming in the sparkling lagoons will make you feel like you've stepped into a postcard-perfect tropical paradise.

Fiji's volcanic landscapes provide yet another layer of wonder for adventurers. The Yasur Volcano on Tanna Island in Vanuatu, though not part of Fiji, is a sight to behold. Witnessing the fiery spectacle of the volcano's eruptions is a once-in-a-lifetime experience that showcases the raw power of nature.

For those who prefer to explore at a slower pace, Fiji's beaches are an invitation to unwind and soak in the natural beauty. The soft white sands and turquoise waters create the perfect backdrop for relaxation and reflection.

Fiji's Coral Reefs: A Diver's Delight

In the shimmering waters of Fiji, a diver's paradise awaits - the captivating coral reefs that adorn the ocean floor. Fiji's coral reefs are renowned worldwide for their pristine beauty, vibrant colors, and teeming marine life. Divers from around the globe flock to these waters, drawn by the allure of exploring one of the most biodiverse and captivating underwater worlds on the planet.

Fiji is home to an extensive network of coral reefs, with the Great Astrolabe Reef standing as one of the world's largest barrier reefs. Spanning over 100 kilometers along the southern coast of Kadavu Island, this majestic reef is a sanctuary for marine life and a haven for divers seeking unforgettable encounters.

The coral formations that grace Fiji's reefs are nothing short of breathtaking. Hard corals, such as staghorn and plate corals, create intricate structures that provide essential shelter and feeding grounds for a myriad of marine creatures. Soft corals, with their delicate and swaying branches, add an ethereal touch to the underwater landscape, while sea fans display their exquisite fan-like patterns, moving gracefully with the ocean currents.

Colorful fish dart among the corals, their vibrant hues creating a mesmerizing underwater ballet. Schools of butterflyfish, angelfish, and parrotfish add splashes of color to the reefs, while elusive creatures, such as the frogfish and leafy seadragon, hide amidst the corals, testing the keen eye of divers to spot them.

Fiji's coral reefs are also a sanctuary for larger marine species. Sharks, including bull sharks and tiger sharks, grace these waters, awe-inspiring yet often misunderstood creatures that play a vital role in maintaining the ecological balance of the reefs.

Manta rays, with their impressive wingspans, glide majestically through the currents, captivating divers with their grace and elegance. These gentle giants often visit cleaning stations on the reefs, where small fish remove parasites from their bodies, creating a fascinating spectacle for lucky observers.

Turtles are another highlight of Fiji's reefs. The islands are home to various turtle species, including hawksbill and green turtles. Divers and snorkelers have the opportunity to encounter these ancient mariners in their natural habitat, witnessing their serene movements as they navigate the underwater landscape.

Fiji's coral reefs are not only a feast for the eyes but also an invaluable ecosystem that supports countless marine organisms. The reefs provide vital nursery grounds for juvenile fish, ensuring the future abundance of marine life. The intricate balance of the reef's biodiversity is a delicate dance that relies on the health and preservation of these underwater habitats.

Fiji's commitment to marine conservation and sustainable tourism practices is evident in its efforts to protect its coral reefs. Marine protected areas have been established to safeguard these delicate ecosystems, and guidelines for responsible diving and snorkeling practices are in place to minimize the impact on the reefs.

The conservation efforts extend beyond Fiji's borders, with international organizations collaborating to protect and preserve the unique biodiversity of the South Pacific region. Fiji's coral reefs are an integral part of this global effort to safeguard the world's underwater wonders.

For divers seeking to immerse themselves in Fiji's coral wonderland, the islands offer a plethora of dive sites catering to all levels of experience. From shallow, calm lagoons for beginners to exhilarating drift dives and underwater caves for the more advanced, Fiji's dive sites promise an adventure of a lifetime.

The Beauty of Fiji's Waterfalls and Rivers

In the heart of Fiji's lush landscapes, a mesmerizing world of waterfalls and rivers awaits, where nature's symphony echoes through the canopies, and pristine waters cascade with breathtaking splendor. Fiji's waterfalls and rivers are a testament to the raw beauty of the islands, inviting travelers to immerse themselves in the serenity and grandeur of this tropical paradise.

Taveuni Island, known as the "Garden Island" of Fiji, boasts some of the most magnificent waterfalls in the region. The Bouma National Heritage Park is home to the Tavoro Waterfalls, a series of three cascades that offer an idyllic setting for relaxation and rejuvenation. Surrounded by lush rainforests, these falls beckon visitors to take a refreshing dip in the crystal-clear pools at their base, creating a postcard-perfect tropical escape.

Fiji's second-largest island, Vanua Levu, is home to the SavuSavu waterfalls, known for their dramatic beauty. The Vuadomo Waterfall, in particular, cascades dramatically into a deep pool, offering an exhilarating experience for those daring enough to take the plunge and swim in its cool waters.

The scenic beauty of Fiji's waterfalls extends beyond the major islands. The stunning Savulevu Yavonu Waterfall on Ovalau Island is a hidden gem, accessible only through a guided hike through verdant landscapes and village plantations. The reward for the journey is the breathtaking sight of the waterfall plunging into a natural pool, surrounded by lush greenery.

Venturing inland, Fiji's rivers offer a different kind of allure. The Navua River, flowing through the heart of Viti Levu, presents a pristine landscape that captivates with every twist and turn. Whitewater rafting down the Navua River is an adventure of a lifetime, taking adventurers through lush rainforests and cascading rapids, all while soaking in the untouched beauty of Fiji's wilderness.

The Sigatoka River, known as Fiji's longest river, offers a serene contrast to the thrill of rafting. A leisurely cruise along the river presents an opportunity to witness Fiji's diverse flora and fauna, including vibrant birdlife and indigenous plants that line the riverbanks.

Fiji's rivers are not only breathtakingly beautiful but also significant to local communities. They serve as essential sources of freshwater for villages, sustaining livelihoods and agricultural activities. The rivers play a vital role in Fijian culture and are often imbued with spiritual significance, a testament to the deep connection between the Fijian people and their natural environment.

Throughout Fiji's islands, visitors have the opportunity to embrace the splendor of these waterfalls and rivers through guided tours and excursions. Local guides share their intimate knowledge of the landscapes and their cultural significance, offering travelers a deeper appreciation of Fiji's natural wonders.

Fiji's commitment to preserving its pristine waterfalls and rivers is evident in its conservation efforts. National parks and protected areas have been established to safeguard these delicate ecosystems, ensuring that future generations can continue to marvel at the untouched beauty of Fiji's wilderness.

Experiencing Fiji's Volcanic Landscapes

In the heart of the South Pacific, Fiji's volcanic landscapes beckon adventurers with their rugged beauty and awe-inspiring allure. These ancient geological wonders paint a picture of a land shaped by the forces of nature, offering travelers a chance to connect with the raw power and timeless beauty of volcanic activity.

The volcanic origins of Fiji's islands are evident in their dramatic terrains, where volcanic cones and craters dot the landscapes, creating a stunning contrast to the lush greenery that thrives in these fertile lands. Many of Fiji's islands were formed through volcanic activity millions of years ago, leaving behind a legacy of rugged mountains and fertile valleys.

The Yasawa Islands, for example, are part of a volcanic archipelago that stretches across Fiji's western coastline. Towering volcanic peaks rise majestically, offering panoramic vistas of the surrounding turquoise waters. Hiking to the summit of these peaks rewards adventurers with breathtaking views of the island chain and the vast expanse of the Pacific Ocean.

Taveuni Island, known as the "Garden Island" of Fiji, boasts the active volcano Mount Uluigalau, Fiji's highest peak. The volcanic soil of Taveuni nurtures lush rainforests and a rich diversity of flora and fauna. Hiking through these dense forests allows visitors to witness firsthand the fertile legacy of volcanic activity.

On Vanua Levu, the second-largest island, the extinct volcano of Mount Koro is another testament to Fiji's volcanic history. The crater of Mount Koro holds a freshwater lake, adding to the island's scenic allure and providing an oasis for nature lovers to explore.

Fiji's volcanic landscapes extend beyond the major islands, with the Ringgold Islands in the Lau Group offering an opportunity to witness volcanic activity underwater. Submerged volcanic calderas and seamounts are havens for marine life, attracting divers and researchers from around the world.

As we delve into Fiji's volcanic landscapes, we discover a land shaped by ancient eruptions, where the fertile soils and rich biodiversity are a testament to the resilience of life in the face of powerful geological forces.

For travelers seeking to experience the volcanic wonders up close, guided tours and hiking expeditions are available, allowing adventurers to explore these rugged terrains safely and responsibly. Local guides offer insights into the geological history and cultural significance of these volcanic sites, enriching the journey with knowledge and appreciation.

Fiji's volcanic landscapes are not only a source of natural beauty but also hold cultural significance for the Fijian people. Volcanoes and volcanic rocks play a role in traditional ceremonies and are considered sacred by local communities.

While Fiji's volcanic activity has been relatively quiet in recent times, the islands' geological history reminds us of the ever-changing nature of our planet. The volcanic landscapes are a testament to the forces that have shaped the world we live in, adding to the allure of Fiji as a destination that embraces both its natural wonders and cultural heritage.

Historic Landmarks: Journey through Fiji's Past

Embark on a journey through Fiji's rich history as we uncover the fascinating historic landmarks that have stood the test of time, preserving the tales of bygone eras. The islands of Fiji have witnessed the footsteps of ancient civilizations, European explorers, and the struggle for independence, each leaving behind a tapestry of heritage waiting to be explored.

The ancient capital of Fiji, Levuka, stands as a living testament to the nation's colonial past. Located on the island of Ovalau, Levuka was Fiji's first colonial capital, serving as the center of governance during British rule. Today, the town's well-preserved colonial architecture harkens back to a bygone era, offering visitors a glimpse into Fiji's early interactions with European explorers and traders.

Another captivating landmark from Fiji's colonial past is the Grand Pacific Hotel in Suva. Built-in 1914, this historic hotel exudes elegance and charm, having hosted dignitaries, royals, and notable figures from around the world. It stands as a symbol of Fiji's hospitality and its significance as a crossroads of cultures.

Delving further into Fiji's history, the ancient archaeological site of Sigatoka Sand Dunes reveals evidence of early human habitation on the islands. These dunes, estimated to be over 3,000 years old, offer a unique insight into the ancient cultures that once thrived in these lands. Excavations have unearthed pottery, tools, and burial sites, providing valuable clues about the early settlers' way of life.

Trekking through the highlands of Viti Levu, the historical village of Navala transports visitors back in time with its traditional thatched-roof bures and simple way of life. The village is home to the distinctive Bure Kalou, a traditional Fijian temple where ancient rituals and ceremonies were once conducted to honor ancestral spirits.

The Sri Siva Subramaniya Temple in Nadi offers a glimpse into Fiji's Indian heritage. Built-in 1986, this stunning temple is a vibrant testament to Fiji's multicultural fabric, reflecting the traditions and beliefs brought to the islands by Indian indentured laborers in the 19th century.

On Taveuni Island, the remains of a once-mighty fortress stand on a hill overlooking the sea. The Vatuwiri Fort, also known as the Bouma Fort, was constructed by Tongan warriors during their occupation of Fiji in the 19th century. Today, it stands as a reminder of the island's turbulent history and the struggles for power that shaped Fiji's past.

As we journey through Fiji's historic landmarks, we uncover stories of conquest, trade, and cultural exchange that have shaped the nation's identity. These landmarks stand as living witnesses to Fiji's complex and multifaceted history, reflecting the resilience and diversity of its people.

Fiji's commitment to preserving its historical heritage is evident in the efforts to protect and maintain these landmarks. Historical preservation initiatives and museums showcase the artifacts and stories of Fiji's past, ensuring that future generations can continue to learn from and appreciate their cultural legacy.

Suva: Capital City and Vibrant Cultural Hub

Nestled along the southeastern coast of Viti Levu, Suva is a melting pot of traditions, where the old and new harmoniously coexist, creating a unique tapestry of experiences for visitors to explore.

Stepping into Suva, the first thing that strikes you is the lively energy that permeates the city. Bustling markets, colorful street vendors, and the sound of laughter and music fill the air, showcasing the Fijian people's warm and welcoming spirit. Suva's diverse population reflects the multicultural fabric of Fiji, with Fijians, Indo-Fijians, Europeans, and other ethnicities coming together to form a harmonious community.

As the political, cultural, and economic center of Fiji, Suva exudes an air of importance and sophistication. The historic Government Buildings, with their striking colonial architecture, stand as an iconic symbol of the nation's governance. Nearby, the ornate Albert Park hosts various cultural events and festivities, adding to the city's vibrancy.

For those seeking to immerse themselves in Fiji's art and history, the Fiji Museum in Suva offers an enriching experience. The museum's exhibits showcase the nation's rich heritage, from ancient artifacts and traditional crafts to contemporary artwork and historical documents, providing a deeper understanding of Fiji's past and present.

Suva's culinary scene is a delightful exploration of flavors and traditions. Local eateries and street vendors offer an array of delectable Fijian dishes, from the iconic lovo (earth oven) feast to delicious Indian curries and tropical fruit delights. Suva's dining experiences cater to all tastes, ensuring that visitors can savor the diverse essence of Fijian cuisine.

The city's nightlife is equally vibrant, with various bars, clubs, and restaurants inviting visitors to dance and celebrate into the night. Live music and cultural performances add to the festive atmosphere, showcasing the beauty of Fijian music, dance, and storytelling.

Suva's cultural attractions extend beyond the city's boundaries. A short drive from Suva leads to the Colo-i-Suva Forest Park, a haven of lush rainforests, cascading waterfalls, and tranquil swimming holes. Nature enthusiasts can embark on hiking trails to immerse themselves in Fiji's natural beauty, just a stone's throw away from the bustling city.

Suva is also home to the University of the South Pacific, drawing students from across the region and beyond, adding to the city's cosmopolitan atmosphere. The university's campus hosts a vibrant community of young minds, contributing to the city's intellectual and artistic endeavors.

The city's central market, known as the Suva Municipal Market, is a hub of activity, where locals gather to buy and sell fresh produce, handicrafts, and cultural artifacts. A visit to the market is an opportunity to interact with the friendly vendors and experience the pulse of everyday life in Suva.

Fiji's commitment to preserving its capital's heritage and environment is evident in various initiatives. Suva's sustainable development plans aim to balance modernization with the preservation of cultural and natural treasures. Efforts to promote eco-friendly practices and community engagement are shaping Suva's future as a vibrant and environmentally conscious city.

Discovering Lautoka: Fiji's Sugar City

Nestled along the northwest coast of Viti Levu, Lautoka is a city of enchantment and industry, earning the moniker "Sugar City" due to its significant role in Fiji's sugar production. As you enter Lautoka, the sweet aroma of sugarcane fills the air, welcoming you to a place where tradition and progress intertwine to create a captivating experience.

Lautoka's history is deeply rooted in its sugar heritage. The city's sugar industry dates back to the late 19th century when sugarcane cultivation and processing became a major economic activity in Fiji. Today, Lautoka's sugar mills remain a vital part of the city's identity, employing many locals and contributing significantly to the nation's economy.

A visit to Lautoka's sugar mill offers a fascinating insight into the sugar production process. During the crushing season, which typically runs from June to November, the mill comes alive with activity as sugarcane is harvested, crushed, and processed into raw sugar. Guided tours allow visitors to witness this age-old process and learn about its importance in Fiji's agricultural history.

Lautoka's cultural diversity is also a defining characteristic of the city. The vibrant marketplace, known as the Lautoka Municipal Market, is a hub of activity where locals from various ethnic backgrounds gather to buy and sell fresh produce, spices, and handmade crafts. A stroll through the market offers a sensory delight of colors, flavors, and friendly interactions with vendors.

One of Lautoka's prominent cultural events is the annual Sugar Festival, held to celebrate the city's sugar heritage. The festival showcases Fijian traditions, such as dance, music, and food, creating a lively atmosphere that draws both locals and visitors to join in the festivities.

Beyond its sugar industry and cultural attractions, Lautoka's natural beauty is equally captivating. The city is surrounded by lush sugarcane fields, creating a picturesque landscape that stretches toward the horizon. Just a short drive from Lautoka leads to the scenic Vuda Point Marina, where azure waters and gentle sea breezes invite relaxation and exploration.

Lautoka is also a gateway to Fiji's renowned Yasawa and Mamanuca Islands, with ferry services departing from nearby Vuda Marina. These idyllic island getaways offer an escape to paradise, with pristine beaches, crystal-clear waters, and vibrant coral reefs for snorkeling and diving.

For those seeking an authentic Fijian experience, Lautoka's traditional Fijian villages offer a glimpse into the warm hospitality and simple way of life that defines rural Fiji. Guided tours allow visitors to participate in traditional ceremonies, taste local delicacies, and learn about the customs and beliefs passed down through generations.

Lautoka's commitment to preserving its natural beauty and cultural heritage is evident in various conservation efforts. The city is part of Fiji's sustainable tourism initiatives, promoting responsible travel practices that protect the environment and support local communities.

Nadi: Gateway to Paradise

Nestled on the western coast of Viti Levu, Fiji's largest island, Nadi is a vibrant city that serves as the primary entry point for travelers exploring the captivating wonders of Fiji. As you step off the plane at Nadi International Airport, you are greeted by the warm tropical breeze and the scent of saltwater in the air. The moment you set foot on this beautiful island, you know you've arrived in a destination like no other, where the promise of adventure and relaxation awaits.

Nadi's strategic location makes it an ideal base for exploring Fiji's famous Mamanuca and Yasawa Islands. Just a short boat ride away from the mainland, these pristine island chains boast crystal-clear waters, palm-fringed beaches, and a wealth of water-based activities, such as snorkeling, diving, and island hopping.

But Nadi itself is much more than just a stopover; it's a destination brimming with its own unique charm and experiences. The city's lively energy is palpable, with its bustling markets, street vendors selling fresh tropical fruits, and colorful storefronts adorned with Fijian handicrafts and souvenirs.

Nadi's multicultural character is evident in its people and cuisine. Indo-Fijian influences are prominent, with a plethora of restaurants offering delicious curries, roti, and other flavorful dishes. The flavors of India meet the tropical abundance of Fiji in a delightful fusion of taste and culture.

One of Nadi's iconic landmarks is the Sri Siva Subramaniya Temple, the largest Hindu temple in the Southern Hemisphere. Its vibrant Dravidian architecture, adorned with intricate carvings and colorful statues, is a sight to behold, drawing visitors from all walks of life to witness its beauty and spirituality.

For those seeking to immerse themselves in Fiji's rich history, the Garden of the Sleeping Giant is a must-visit attraction. This botanical sanctuary, once owned by actor Raymond Burr, showcases a collection of exotic orchids and native plants, providing a serene escape into Fiji's natural beauty.

Nadi's golden beaches, such as Wailoaloa Beach, are perfect for unwinding and soaking in the sunsets over the Pacific Ocean. Adventure seekers can partake in thrilling activities like jet skiing, parasailing, and paddleboarding, adding a dose of excitement to their tropical getaway.

Beyond the city's vibrant offerings, Nadi is home to various cultural events and festivals that celebrate Fiji's heritage. The annual Bula Festival is a lively affair, featuring parades, dances, and cultural performances that bring the community together to showcase their customs and traditions.

Nadi's commitment to sustainability and eco-conscious practices is reflected in various initiatives, including eco-tourism efforts and community-driven projects that preserve the city's natural beauty and support the livelihoods of local communities.

As the sun sets over Nadi, the city's nightlife comes alive with various bars, restaurants, and resorts offering evening entertainment. Fijian cultural shows and fire dancing performances add to the vibrant atmosphere, allowing visitors to immerse themselves in the rhythms and rituals of the South Pacific.

Nadi's charm lies in its ability to be both a bustling city and a tranquil paradise, catering to every traveler's desires. Whether you seek adventure, relaxation, or cultural immersion, Nadi stands as the perfect gateway to your Fijian escapade.

Exploring Savusavu: Fiji's Hidden Gem

Nestled along the southern coast of Vanua Levu, Fiji's second-largest island, lies the enchanting town of Savusavu. Often referred to as Fiji's "Hidden Gem," Savusavu is a haven of natural beauty, tranquility, and warm hospitality, inviting travelers to experience a slice of paradise away from the hustle and bustle of modern life.

As you arrive in Savusavu, you'll immediately feel the serene ambiance that permeates the air. The town's picturesque setting, surrounded by lush green hills and glistening blue waters, creates a sense of calm that washes over you like a gentle breeze. Savusavu is a place where time seems to slow down, allowing visitors to savor each moment in this tranquil oasis.

One of Savusavu's most notable attractions is its natural harbor, which is often called the "Hidden Paradise of Fiji." The Savusavu Bay is not only a safe haven for sailors, but it also offers mesmerizing views of the surrounding landscapes. Watching the sunset over the bay is a moment of pure magic, as the sky transforms into a canvas of vivid hues.

The charm of Savusavu lies in its authentic Fijian atmosphere. The town is relatively untouched by mass tourism, allowing travelers to immerse themselves in the genuine warmth and friendliness of the locals. Savusavu's residents are known for their genuine hospitality, making visitors feel like they're part of the community from the moment they arrive.

Savusavu is also known for its thriving arts and crafts scene. The town's market, bustling with vibrant colors and sounds, showcases an array of handmade products, from intricate wooden carvings to delicate textiles and exquisite jewelry. Exploring the market is a delightful way to support local artisans and take home a piece of Fiji's rich cultural heritage.

The coastal town is a gateway to a myriad of nature-based adventures. The surrounding rainforests and rugged landscapes offer fantastic opportunities for hiking and trekking, rewarding adventurers with breathtaking vistas and encounters with Fiji's unique flora and fauna.

One of the most famous natural wonders near Savusavu is the enchanting Bouma National Heritage Park on Taveuni Island. This protected area boasts a network of walking trails, leading to cascading waterfalls, crystal-clear pools, and ancient volcanic craters, making it a must-visit destination for nature enthusiasts.

Savusavu's marine life is equally captivating. The Savusavu Bay and surrounding waters are a paradise for divers and snorkelers, offering a kaleidoscope of colorful coral reefs and diverse marine species. The soft coral capital of the world, Savusavu's underwater world is teeming with life, making it a dream destination for diving enthusiasts.

For those seeking a relaxing escape, Savusavu is home to various luxurious resorts and spa retreats, where guests can indulge in rejuvenating treatments while being surrounded by Fiji's natural beauty. The slow pace of life in Savusavu encourages travelers to unwind, de-stress, and embrace a sense of inner peace.

As the sun sets over Savusavu, the town comes alive with cultural performances and local celebrations, providing an opportunity to experience the traditional music, dance, and storytelling that have been passed down through generations.

Savusavu's commitment to sustainable tourism is evident in various eco-friendly initiatives. Local efforts focus on preserving the pristine environment, supporting local communities, and ensuring that visitors can experience Fiji's hidden gem while minimizing their impact on this delicate paradise.

Taveuni: The Garden Island of Fiji

Welcome to Taveuni, the lush and picturesque "Garden Island" of Fiji. Located in the northern part of the archipelago, Taveuni is a paradise that captivates with its stunning landscapes, pristine wilderness, and vibrant biodiversity, earning its reputation as one of Fiji's most captivating destinations.

As you step onto Taveuni's shores, you're greeted by the sweet scent of blooming flowers and the melodic chirping of tropical birds. The island's verdant beauty immediately surrounds you, beckoning you to explore its natural wonders and immerse yourself in the serenity of this garden-like paradise.

Taveuni is renowned for its rich flora and fauna, earning the title of "The Garden Island" for good reason. The island is a haven of rare and exotic plant species, many of which are endemic to the region. The Taveuni forests are a treasure trove of botanical diversity, with orchids, ferns, and colorful blossoms adorning the landscape like a living tapestry.

At the heart of Taveuni lies the Bouma National Heritage Park, a pristine protected area that covers nearly 80% of the island. This natural sanctuary offers a network of hiking trails, leading to majestic waterfalls, volcanic craters, and hidden swimming holes, all surrounded by lush rainforests. The Tavoro Waterfalls, in particular, are a sight to behold, with their cascading waters inviting visitors to take a refreshing dip in their crystal-clear pools.

Taveuni's underwater realm is equally breathtaking. The surrounding waters are teeming with marine life, making it a diver's paradise. The Rainbow Reef, part of the Somosomo Strait, is famous for its vibrant soft coral gardens, earning it the title of "Soft Coral Capital of the World." Snorkeling and scuba diving in these pristine waters offer a kaleidoscope of colors and a chance to encounter a rich array of marine species, including reef sharks, manta rays, and colorful tropical fish.

Taveuni's pristine environment is protected by the people's dedication to conservation and sustainable practices. The local communities are actively involved in preserving the island's natural beauty, making eco-tourism a significant focus for the island's economy. Visitors to Taveuni can immerse themselves in eco-friendly experiences that support the local communities and protect the island's delicate ecosystems.

Away from the natural wonders, Taveuni offers opportunities to experience Fiji's traditional way of life. The island's friendly residents welcome visitors with warm hospitality, providing a chance to witness the genuine Fijian spirit and immerse themselves in the local customs and traditions.

Fiji's cultural heritage is celebrated on Taveuni through various festivals and ceremonies. The annual Taveuni Day celebration showcases Fijian music, dance, and culinary delights, allowing visitors to partake in the festivities and experience the island's rich cultural tapestry.

Taveuni is also home to the International Date Line, offering a unique geographical feature that allows travelers to stand with one foot in the present and the other in the future, symbolizing the timeless allure of this extraordinary island.

Taveuni's allure lies in its ability to transport visitors to a world of unspoiled beauty and natural wonders. Whether hiking through the rainforests, exploring the underwater realm, or basking in the warm embrace of Fijian culture, Taveuni promises an unforgettable journey of discovery and rejuvenation.

The Mamanuca and Yasawa Islands: Tropical Escapes

The Mamanuca Islands, a stunning archipelago located just west of the main island of Viti Levu, are a collection of twenty captivating islets, each boasting its own unique charm. These islands are easily accessible from Nadi, Fiji's international gateway, making them a popular destination for both day-trippers and luxury-seeking travelers.

The Mamanucas are renowned for their postcard-perfect white sandy beaches and azure waters, making them a haven for sun-worshippers and water sports enthusiasts. Snorkeling, scuba diving, and surfing opportunities abound, with vibrant coral reefs and abundant marine life awaiting exploration beneath the waves.

Popular Mamanuca Islands like Malolo, Mana, and Castaway offer a range of luxurious resorts, boutique hotels, and budget-friendly accommodations, catering to every traveler's preferences. Whether you seek a romantic honeymoon escape or a fun-filled family vacation, the Mamanuca Islands have something to offer for everyone.

For adventure seekers, a visit to Cloud 9, a floating bar and restaurant located in the middle of the ocean, is a must. Here, guests can indulge in refreshing cocktails, tasty wood-fired pizzas, and stunning panoramic views of the surrounding waters. The relaxed atmosphere and floating platform create an unforgettable experience that embodies the essence of Fiji's laid-back island vibe.

Continuing north from the Mamanucas, you'll find the Yasawa Islands, a more remote and untouched paradise, consisting of a string of volcanic islands with rugged landscapes and secluded beaches. The Yasawas are less developed than their neighboring Mamanucas, offering a more off-the-beaten-path experience for intrepid travelers.

The Yasawa Islands are perfect for those seeking a back-to-nature experience, with opportunities for hiking, village visits, and cultural exchanges with the local Fijian communities. Traditional Fijian villages on these islands offer a chance to witness authentic Fijian customs and rituals, showcasing the warm hospitality and rich heritage of the Yasawan people.

Among the many breathtaking sights in the Yasawas is the famous Sawa-i-Lau Caves, a hidden gem of the South Pacific. These magnificent limestone caves can only be accessed by swimming through an underwater passage, adding to the sense of adventure and mystique. Once inside, the caves reveal a stunning chamber with crystal-clear waters, where visitors can swim and bask in the natural beauty of this unique wonder.

The Mamanuca and Yasawa Islands have played starring roles in numerous films and television shows, including the famous movie "Cast Away" starring Tom Hanks. Their cinematic appeal lies in their pristine landscapes and dreamlike beauty, which have captured the imaginations of travelers and filmmakers alike.

Both island groups are easily accessible by boat, and island-hopping tours are a popular way to explore their hidden coves and secluded beaches. Travelers can tailor their island-hopping experiences to suit their preferences, whether seeking relaxation, adventure, or a combination of both.

The Mamanuca and Yasawa Islands are an embodiment of Fiji's tropical paradise, offering a dreamlike escape from the ordinary and a chance to embrace the serenity and natural beauty of the South Pacific. Whether savoring the warm sun on soft sandy beaches, snorkeling in clear waters teeming with marine life, or immersing in the rich Fijian culture, these island groups promise an unforgettable tropical getaway like no other.

Viti Levu: Fiji's Largest and Most Diverse Island

Viti Levu is the economic and political center of Fiji, home to the bustling capital city of Suva, as well as Nadi, the primary gateway for international travelers. Its strategic location and accessibility make it a hub for both tourists and locals, offering a diverse array of attractions and activities that cater to every taste and preference.

The island's interior is dominated by the rugged peaks of the Central Range, a majestic mountain range that stretches across the heart of Viti Levu. Mount Tomanivi, Fiji's highest peak, towers above at an impressive 4,344 feet (1,324 meters), offering adventurous trekkers the opportunity to hike to its summit and be rewarded with breathtaking panoramic views of the island's lush interior.

The Coral Coast, located on the southern shores of Viti Levu, is famous for its stunning beaches and crystal-clear waters. Resorts and hotels line the coast, providing visitors with opportunities to bask in the sun, snorkel in vibrant coral reefs, and witness awe-inspiring sunsets that paint the sky in hues of orange and pink.

Suva, Fiji's capital city, is a vibrant cultural hub that showcases the island's dynamic fusion of traditions. The city is a melting pot of cultures, with a rich blend of Fijian, Indian, Chinese, and European influences that shape its architecture, cuisine, and way of life. The Fiji Museum in Suva offers a captivating journey through the island's history, showcasing artifacts, artwork, and exhibits that highlight Fiji's past and present.

Nadi, on the western coast of Viti Levu, is the main gateway for international travelers arriving in Fiji. This bustling town is a bustling melting pot of cultures, offering a wide range of restaurants, shops, and markets where visitors can indulge in authentic Fijian cuisine and shop for traditional handicrafts and souvenirs.

Viti Levu's rich cultural heritage is celebrated through various festivals and events, such as the Bula Festival and the Hibiscus Festival, which bring the community together to showcase their customs, music, dance, and culinary delights. These vibrant celebrations provide an opportunity for travelers to immerse themselves in the warmth and hospitality of the Fijian people.

The island's natural wonders extend beyond its beaches and mountains. Viti Levu is home to a variety of picturesque waterfalls, including the enchanting Tavoro Waterfalls in Bouma National Heritage Park. These cascading wonders offer a refreshing respite and a chance to connect with Fiji's lush rainforest landscapes.

For those seeking adventure, the Navua River offers thrilling white-water rafting experiences, allowing adrenaline junkies to navigate through exhilarating rapids amidst pristine rainforest scenery.

Viti Levu's interior is also rich in cultural significance, with various traditional villages providing visitors with opportunities to experience Fijian customs and rituals first-hand. Visits to these villages offer a chance to witness age-old practices, such as Kava ceremonies and meke performances, which celebrate Fiji's proud cultural heritage.

The island's commitment to eco-tourism is evident in various conservation efforts and community-driven initiatives that aim to protect its delicate ecosystems and preserve its unique biodiversity. Travelers can partake in eco-friendly experiences that support the island's environment and communities, ensuring that future generations can continue to enjoy Viti Levu's natural beauty.

Viti Levu's allure lies in its remarkable diversity, offering travelers a taste of every aspect of Fiji's enchanting appeal. Whether exploring the vibrant city life, trekking through majestic mountains, or delving into the island's cultural tapestry, Viti Levu promises an unforgettable journey that embodies the spirit of Fiji's largest and most diverse island.

Vanua Levu: Fiji's Northern Treasure

As Fiji's second-largest island, Vanua Levu offers a refreshing escape from the bustling tourist crowds, providing a more laid-back and tranquil experience for those seeking a deeper connection with nature and the Fijian way of life.

Vanua Levu is less developed than its southern counterpart, Viti Levu, allowing travelers to immerse themselves in a genuine Fijian experience that has retained its authenticity over the years. The island's lush rainforests, meandering rivers, and rugged mountain ranges create a picturesque backdrop for an adventure like no other.

The town of Savusavu, located on the southern coast of Vanua Levu, serves as the island's main hub for travelers. Known for its natural harbor and welcoming atmosphere, Savusavu is a popular destination for sailors, divers, and adventurers alike. The town's relaxed ambiance and warm-hearted locals make it a delightful place to begin your journey into the heart of Vanua Levu.

For those seeking an intimate encounter with nature, the Natewa Bay, located on the northeastern coast of the island, offers a sanctuary of biodiversity. This pristine bay is home to diverse marine life, making it a haven for snorkelers and scuba divers. The Natewa Bay Conservation Area, encompassing over 30,000 acres, protects critical habitats, including the Great Sea Reef, which is the third-largest barrier reef in the world.

Venturing inland, travelers will find themselves surrounded by Vanua Levu's untamed wilderness. The Wasali Nature Reserve, located near Savusavu, is a haven for birdwatchers and nature enthusiasts, offering a chance to spot rare and endemic bird species amidst the lush rainforest.

For a taste of authentic Fijian village life, a visit to the Nukubalavu Village is a must. Here, you can witness traditional ceremonies, learn about ancient customs, and partake in a Kava ceremony, an integral part of Fijian culture. The warm hospitality of the villagers will make you feel like a cherished member of their community.

Vanua Levu's more remote regions, such as the southeast and northwestern coasts, offer secluded beaches and tranquil retreats where visitors can unwind and connect with nature. Resorts and eco-lodges in these areas provide an eco-conscious escape that supports local communities and protects the island's natural beauty.

One of the highlights of Vanua Levu is the Labasa Town, located on the northern coast. Known for its vibrant markets and sugar cane fields, Labasa provides an authentic glimpse into the island's agricultural traditions. The friendly locals and bustling atmosphere make it an ideal place to soak in the Fijian way of life.

Vanua Levu's charm lies in its ability to transport visitors to a world untouched by time, where the spirit of Fiji's traditions and natural beauty come together in perfect harmony. This northern treasure invites travelers to embark on a journey of exploration, where each moment brings new wonders and enriching experiences that leave a lasting impression.

Getting Around Fiji: Transportation and Tips

Navigating the enchanting islands of Fiji is an adventure in itself, where the journey becomes as memorable as the destination. In this chapter, we'll explore the various modes of transportation available in Fiji, providing you with essential tips to ensure a seamless and enjoyable travel experience.

Domestic Flights: Fiji is well-connected by domestic flights, making it convenient to hop between the islands. The two main domestic airlines are Fiji Airways and Fiji Link. Nadi International Airport and Nausori International Airport (near Suva) serve as the main domestic flight hubs.

Ferries and Boats: Ferries and boats are the lifelines of inter-island travel in Fiji. The ferries are a popular and budget-friendly way to explore the Mamanuca and Yasawa Islands, providing picturesque journeys across the sparkling Pacific waters.

Water Taxis: Water taxis offer a more flexible and personalized option for island-hopping. They provide door-to-door service, allowing you to explore hidden coves and remote beaches at your own pace.

Rental Cars: For those looking to explore Viti Levu and Vanua Levu independently, renting a car is a convenient option. The roads in these regions are generally well-maintained, but driving conditions may vary on some rural roads.

Buses: Buses are the most common mode of transportation on the larger islands. The local buses are an affordable and authentic way to travel, allowing you to interact with the friendly locals and experience Fiji's culture firsthand.

Taxis: Taxis are readily available in major towns and cities. They are metered, and it's a good idea to check the fare before starting your journey. In some remote areas, shared taxis (minivans) provide transportation between villages.

Rental Bicycles: Some resorts and eco-lodges offer rental bicycles, providing a fun and eco-friendly way to explore the nearby areas.

Seaplanes and Helicopters: For a truly luxurious experience, seaplanes and helicopters offer scenic flights over Fiji's stunning landscapes, giving you a bird's-eye view of the islands' beauty.

Tips for Getting Around Fiji:

Plan Ahead: Research and plan your transportation options in advance, especially for inter-island travel. Some ferries and flights have limited schedules, so booking early is recommended.

Be Flexible: In Fiji, things may not always run on strict schedules. Embrace the laid-back island time mentality and be flexible with your travel plans.

Respect Local Customs: When using public transportation, remember to dress modestly and remove your shoes before boarding buses or entering someone's home.

Pack Lightly: Traveling around the islands often involves small boats and planes, so packing lightly with essentials is advisable.

Budget Wisely: While some modes of transportation, such as buses, are budget-friendly, others like seaplanes can be quite expensive. Plan your transportation budget accordingly.

Be Weather-Wise: Tropical weather can be unpredictable, especially during cyclone season (November to April). Stay informed about weather conditions and potential disruptions to travel plans.

Carry Cash: While major towns and cities have ATMs, some remote areas may not, so carry enough cash for your journey.

Embrace the Journey: Traveling in Fiji is about more than just getting from one place to another. Embrace the scenic journeys, connect with the locals, and savor the moments that make Fiji a truly special destination.

By understanding the transportation options and following these tips, you'll be well-prepared to embark on an unforgettable adventure, navigating Fiji's captivating beauty and immersing yourself in the warm embrace of its unique culture and hospitality.

Indigenous Language of Fiji: Fijian and Its Dialects

In the vibrant tapestry of Fiji's cultural heritage, language plays a pivotal role, weaving together the stories, customs, and traditions of the indigenous Fijian people. The main indigenous language of Fiji is Fijian, a rich and expressive language that reflects the island's deep-rooted history and diverse communities.

Fijian, also known as Vosa Vakaviti, is an Austronesian language belonging to the Malayo-Polynesian subgroup. It is part of the larger Oceanic language family, which encompasses the languages spoken across the Pacific islands.

1. The Fijian Language: Fijian is one of the three official languages of Fiji, alongside English and Fiji Hindi. It holds significant cultural importance and is widely spoken by the indigenous iTaukei people. While English is commonly used in official and business settings, Fijian remains the language of daily communication within Fijian communities.

2. Dialects: Within the Fijian language, several dialects exist due to geographical variations and historical influences. The main dialects include Standard Fijian, Eastern Fijian, Western Fijian, and Bauan Fijian. The Standard Fijian dialect is widely understood and serves as a lingua franca among different Fijian-speaking communities.

3. The Bauan Influence: The Bauan dialect holds particular significance in Fiji's history. Bau, an island located off the coast of Viti Levu, was the center of political power during the early colonial era. The Bauan dialect gained prominence and became a unifying language, helping to bridge communication among different Fijian tribes.

4. Written Form: Fijian was traditionally an oral language, and its written form was established during the colonial era when Christian missionaries developed the Fijian alphabet. Today, Fijian is written using the Latin script, which has helped preserve and promote its literature and cultural heritage.

---

5. Importance of Language: Language is deeply intertwined with Fijian identity and cultural preservation. It serves as a vessel for passing down ancestral knowledge, myths, and oral traditions from one generation to the next, fostering a strong sense of community and belonging among the indigenous people.

6. Cultural Expressions: Fijian language and its dialects are integral to various cultural expressions, such as storytelling, music, dance, and traditional ceremonies. Through meke performances and chants, the Fijian language breathes life into captivating stories of ancient warriors, love stories, and legends.

7. Language Revitalization: Efforts are underway to promote and revitalize the Fijian language, especially among the younger generations. Schools and community organizations play a crucial role in preserving the language and ensuring its continuity.

8. Multilingualism in Fiji: Fiji's multicultural society is a testament to the coexistence of different languages. While Fijian is the main indigenous language, Fiji Hindi, an Indo-Aryan language, is widely spoken by the Indo-Fijian community, descendants of indentured laborers brought to Fiji during British colonial times.

9. Embracing Language Diversity: The diverse linguistic landscape of Fiji fosters an environment of tolerance and appreciation for different cultures. Multilingualism is celebrated, and many Fijians are adept at speaking multiple languages, creating a rich tapestry of communication.

In conclusion, the Fijian language and its dialects form an integral part of Fiji's cultural identity, connecting the past with the present and ensuring the preservation of indigenous traditions. As we continue our journey through Fiji's rich heritage, let us cherish the significance of language in shaping the unique and colorful mosaic of this South Pacific paradise.

Communicating in Fiji: Common Phrases and Etiquette

As you journey through the enchanting islands of Fiji, you'll find that connecting with the locals through language is a beautiful way to immerse yourself in the culture and foster meaningful interactions. In this chapter, we'll explore some common Fijian phrases and essential etiquette tips to help you communicate with warmth and respect during your stay.

1. Greetings and Politeness: Politeness is highly valued in Fijian culture. When meeting someone, a warm "Bula!" is the most common and universal greeting. Use "Ni sa bula" for "Good morning" and "Ni sa yadra" for "Good evening." Adding "Vinaka" (thank you) and "Vinaka vakalevu" (thank you very much) when appropriate shows appreciation and courtesy.

2. Introducing Yourself: To introduce yourself, say "O ni sa qai yacova?" which means "What's your name?" Respond with "Au yacova ___" and fill in your name. When meeting elders or chiefs, it is customary to add "Noqu na Turaga" (my Lord/Lady) before their name as a sign of respect.

3. Basic Phrases: Learning some basic Fijian phrases will go a long way in making connections with locals. Use "Yadra" for "Good morning," "Sota tale" for "Goodbye," "Yadra Vinaka" for "Good morning and goodbye," and "Moce" for "Goodnight."

4. Asking for Help: If you need assistance, "I toso" means "Help me." Locals are generally friendly and willing to lend a helping hand.

5. Table Manners: During meals, it's customary to wait for everyone to be seated and for the host to begin before eating. When offered food or drink, it's polite to accept, even if just a small amount.

6. Accepting Kava: Kava is a traditional Fijian drink made from the kava plant's root. When offered kava during a ceremony or gathering, clap once, say "Bula," drink the

kava in one go, and clap three times. Avoid saying "no" when offered kava, as it is seen as disrespectful.

7. Removing Shoes: When entering someone's home or a Fijian village, it's customary to remove your shoes as a sign of respect.

8. Physical Contact: Fijians are generally affectionate and may show warmth through handshakes, hugs, or touching shoulders. Embrace these gestures with an open heart, but always be mindful of personal boundaries.

9. Pointing and Feet: Pointing at people or objects with your finger is considered impolite. Instead, use an open hand gesture. Avoid pointing the soles of your feet at others, as this is seen as disrespectful.

10. Modesty in Dress: In rural or traditional areas, dressing modestly is appreciated. Avoid wearing revealing clothing in villages or during religious ceremonies.

11. Learning the Language: Fijians appreciate visitors who make an effort to learn some basic Fijian phrases. Even if your pronunciation isn't perfect, your attempt will be warmly received.

12. Handshakes and Tipping: Handshakes are common greetings in Fiji, especially in urban areas. Tipping is not a common practice in Fiji, as many establishments include a service charge in the bill.

By embracing these common phrases and observing local etiquette, you'll find that Fijians will warmly welcome you into their community. Your efforts to connect through language and respect for their customs will enrich your experience as you explore the beauty and warmth of the Fijian culture.

Fijian Arts: Music, Dance, and Storytelling

In the heart of Fiji's vibrant cultural tapestry lies a captivating world of artistic expression, where music, dance, and storytelling intertwine to celebrate the rich heritage and ancestral wisdom of the Fijian people. Let us immerse ourselves in the enchanting realm of Fijian arts, where every beat of the drum and graceful movement tells a tale of resilience, love, and the beauty of life.

Music in Fiji holds a profound significance, serving as a rhythmic storyteller that echoes the spirit of the islands. Traditional Fijian music is characterized by the use of indigenous instruments like the lali drum, a large wooden slit drum that plays a vital role in communicating important messages within the community. The pulsating beat of the lali drum marks the beginning of ceremonies, celebrations, and communal gatherings, uniting the Fijian people in harmony.

Accompanying the rhythmic beats of the lali are the melodic sounds of the vakamalolo, a wooden flute, and the dabe or derua, a type of bamboo percussion instrument. The combination of these instruments creates a melodious symphony that captures the essence of Fijian life.

One of the most celebrated Fijian art forms is dance, where movements reflect the grace, strength, and storytelling traditions of the islands. Meke, a traditional dance performed on special occasions, showcases the elegance and prowess of Fijian culture. Dancers don vibrant costumes, adorned with tapa cloth and magimagi (coconut fiber), as they fluidly glide, stomp, and sway to the mesmerizing beats of the music.

The meke incorporates various dance styles, each carrying its significance. The "meke vakamalolo" embodies the movements of the vakamalolo flute, imitating birds and the sway of trees. The "meke taralala" mimics the actions of warriors in battle, evoking a powerful display of strength and unity.

Another enchanting dance is the "meke lako," a farewell dance performed when saying goodbye to visitors or loved ones. As the dancers gracefully sway, they express the heartfelt emotions of parting while conveying blessings for safe journeys.

76

Fijian storytelling, known as "talanoa," is a cherished tradition passed down through generations. Elders and wise storytellers share myths, legends, and historical tales that illuminate the essence of Fijian identity. These tales are not only a source of entertainment but also a means of preserving cultural heritage and imparting valuable life lessons.

Through "talanoa," Fijians learn about their ancestors' bravery, the gods' mysteries, and the island's enchanting creation stories. The oral tradition of storytelling fosters a deep connection to the past, emphasizing the importance of community, family, and the interwoven tapestry of nature and humanity.

Fijian arts are more than mere performances; they are a testament to the profound relationship between the people and their ancestral roots. The dances and stories honor the spirits of the land, sea, and sky, paying tribute to the wisdom of the elders and the dreams of the young.

The arts in Fiji play a crucial role in building a strong sense of cultural pride and unity among the Fijian people. They are a window into the soul of the islands, where the rhythm of the drums, the elegance of the dance, and the power of the stories convey the timeless spirit of Fiji's captivating culture.

Sports and Recreation in Fiji: Rugby and Beyond

In the heart of the South Pacific lies an island nation where sports and recreation play an integral role in the lives of its people. Fiji, a country known for its breathtaking beauty and warm hospitality, boasts a strong sporting culture that centers around its national obsession: rugby. Beyond the rugby fields, a diverse array of recreational activities and traditional sports offer locals and visitors alike an opportunity to connect with the land, sea, and each other in a spirit of camaraderie and joy.

Rugby is more than just a sport in Fiji; it is a way of life that unites communities and fosters national pride. The passion for rugby is ingrained in Fijian culture, with children playing the sport from a young age, often with little more than a makeshift ball and a patch of grass. Rugby transcends social boundaries, bringing together people from all walks of life, and the sport is played in villages, schools, and urban centers across the country.

Fijian rugby players are renowned worldwide for their skill, strength, and flair on the field. Many Fijian players have achieved international success, earning spots in top rugby leagues around the world. The Fiji national rugby team, known as the Flying Fijians, is a source of immense national pride, and their electrifying performances in international tournaments inspire the nation and the global rugby community.

Beyond rugby, the waters surrounding Fiji offer an array of aquatic sports and activities. Water sports enthusiasts can indulge in snorkeling, scuba diving, surfing, and paddleboarding, immersing themselves in the vibrant marine life and pristine coral reefs. The turquoise lagoons and clear waters provide an ideal playground for aquatic adventures.

Sailing is also popular in Fiji, with regattas and yacht races attracting sailors from around the world. The annual Fiji Regatta Week in September is a highlight on the sailing calendar, offering a mix of competitive racing and festive onshore activities.

On land, hiking and trekking enthusiasts can explore the lush tropical rainforests, cascading waterfalls, and volcanic landscapes.

Taveuni, known as the "Garden Island," offers breathtaking trails that lead to hidden gems, such as the Bouma National Heritage Park and the famous Tavoro Waterfalls.

Traditional Fijian sports and games are deeply rooted in the island's history and cultural heritage. "Lau leke" is a Fijian game that involves throwing a large, heavy wooden disc as far as possible, while "kilikiti" is a form of cricket with a Fijian twist, played with a wooden bat and a ball made from pandanus leaves. These traditional sports connect the modern generation with the customs and games of their ancestors.

In Fiji, sports and recreation are not just about competition; they are about forming bonds and celebrating the spirit of unity. "Sevusevu," a traditional welcoming ceremony, often precedes sports events, fostering an atmosphere of respect and togetherness. Sports bring people together, providing an opportunity for communities to celebrate their cultural identity and showcase their talents on a global stage.

As you explore Fiji's sports and recreational offerings, you'll discover that it is not merely a destination but a way of life. Whether you're a rugby enthusiast, a water sports adventurer, or a seeker of traditional experiences, Fiji offers a plethora of opportunities to embrace the island's love for sports, immerse yourself in the warm embrace of the culture, and create memories that will last a lifetime.

Health and Wellness in Fiji: Traditional Practices

In the picturesque landscapes of Fiji, health and wellness are deeply interconnected with the island's natural abundance and ancient knowledge passed down through generations. Traditional Fijian practices have long been at the core of maintaining physical, mental, and spiritual well-being, offering a holistic approach that harmonizes with nature and fosters a sense of community and balance.

One of the cornerstones of Fijian traditional health practices is the use of medicinal plants and herbs. The islands' lush rainforests and fertile soil nurture a diverse array of flora with medicinal properties. Traditional healers, known as "bete," possess invaluable knowledge about these plants and their healing properties. They have been practicing traditional medicine for centuries, treating various ailments and promoting overall wellness.

Herbal remedies are commonly used to alleviate common ailments such as colds, stomach issues, and skin conditions. Traditional healers create poultices, teas, and infusions from plants like kawakawa, noni, and dilo, which are known for their medicinal properties. These natural remedies are believed to have powerful healing effects, and their usage is deeply ingrained in the Fijian way of life.

In addition to herbal remedies, massage therapy, known as "vitalotu," is an integral part of Fijian wellness practices. The healing touch of skilled masseuses helps relieve muscle tension, reduce stress, and improve circulation. Vitalotu techniques, passed down through generations, combine firm pressure with rhythmic movements, promoting a sense of relaxation and rejuvenation.

The Fijian practice of "lovo," a traditional method of cooking, also plays a role in promoting health and well-being. Lovo involves cooking food in an earth oven, where the food is wrapped in banana leaves and placed on hot stones covered with soil. This slow and gentle cooking method preserves the nutrients and flavors of the ingredients, resulting in wholesome and nourishing meals.

Fijian traditional practices also extend to mental and spiritual wellness. Ceremonies, rituals, and cultural gatherings play a vital role in nurturing the spirit and fostering a sense of belonging within the community. "Tambua," or the kava ceremony, is a traditional gathering where the community comes together to share kava, a beverage made from the kava plant's roots. The ceremony promotes bonding, fosters a sense of unity, and serves as a means of communication between the living and the spirits of the ancestors.

The concept of "vanua," which translates to "land" or "home," is deeply ingrained in Fijian culture and is closely tied to the idea of wellness. The land is not merely a physical space but a spiritual entity that provides sustenance and a sense of belonging. The practice of "sevusevu," where visitors seek permission from the land's spirits before entering, reflects the reverence and respect for the environment and its vital role in the well-being of the community.

Beyond traditional practices, modern health care services are available in Fiji, with hospitals, clinics, and medical facilities located in urban centers and major islands. The Fijian government and various organizations work together to provide accessible health care to all citizens and visitors.

Fiji's traditional practices and modern health care blend harmoniously, offering a holistic approach to well-being that embraces the wisdom of the past while adapting to the needs of the present. As you immerse yourself in the beauty of Fiji, take the time to appreciate the interconnectedness of health, nature, and culture, and let the island's traditional practices and warm hospitality guide you on a journey of wellness and rejuvenation.

Education in Fiji: A Path to Empowerment

Education is a cornerstone of society, shaping the future of nations and empowering individuals to thrive in an ever-changing world. In Fiji, education holds immense significance, as it plays a vital role in nurturing the next generation of leaders and equipping them with the knowledge and skills to contribute to their communities and the global stage.

Formal education in Fiji follows a structure of early childhood education, primary education, secondary education, and tertiary education. Early childhood education provides a strong foundation for young learners, fostering cognitive, social, and emotional development. Preschools and kindergartens across the islands offer a nurturing environment where children can explore, learn, and grow.

At the primary education level, Fijian children attend primary schools, where they acquire essential literacy, numeracy, and foundational knowledge. The government of Fiji places great emphasis on providing access to quality education for all children, and primary education is compulsory and free in Fiji.

Secondary education builds upon the knowledge gained in primary school and prepares students for further studies or vocational training. Secondary schools offer a diverse curriculum that includes academic subjects, technical education, and life skills development. Students have the option to pursue academic pathways leading to university entrance or vocational pathways that equip them with practical skills for various careers.

In Fiji, English is the medium of instruction in schools, but Fijian and Hindi are also taught as subjects. This reflects the multicultural nature of Fiji, where various ethnic groups coexist harmoniously and maintain their languages and traditions.

Education in Fiji is not limited to formal classroom settings. The islands' rich cultural heritage is also preserved and transmitted through informal and non-formal education. Traditional knowledge, including storytelling, dance, music, and craftsmanship, is passed down through generations, fostering a deep connection to the land, culture, and community.

Tertiary education in Fiji is provided by universities and vocational institutions. The University of the South Pacific, with campuses in Fiji and other Pacific countries, offers a wide range of programs, attracting students from across the region. Vocational training institutions provide specialized training in areas such as agriculture, trades, and hospitality, catering to the diverse needs of Fiji's workforce.

The Fijian government places significant emphasis on the importance of education and invests in infrastructure, resources, and teacher training to enhance the quality of education across the country. The Ministry of Education ensures that educational policies and programs are inclusive, equitable, and aligned with national development goals.

Beyond formal education, Fiji places value on lifelong learning and adult education programs. These initiatives cater to individuals who missed out on formal education opportunities and seek to upskill or acquire new knowledge and qualifications.

Education in Fiji fosters a sense of national identity and promotes values such as respect, tolerance, and environmental stewardship. Students are encouraged to appreciate and celebrate their cultural heritage while embracing global perspectives. The education system instills a sense of responsibility towards the preservation of Fiji's natural resources and cultural traditions for future generations.

Empowerment through education extends beyond academic achievements. Education equips individuals with critical thinking skills, problem-solving abilities, and adaptability, enabling them to face the challenges of the modern world with resilience and creativity.

Conservation Efforts: Protecting Fiji's Ecosystems

In the heart of the South Pacific lies a paradise of biodiversity and natural wonders: Fiji. With its lush rainforests, pristine coral reefs, and diverse marine life, Fiji is a treasure trove of ecological riches. However, like many island nations, Fiji faces environmental challenges that threaten its delicate ecosystems. In response, dedicated conservation efforts have emerged, driven by both local communities and international organizations, to safeguard Fiji's unique natural heritage for future generations.

One of the most critical aspects of conservation in Fiji is protecting its marine ecosystems, including its extensive coral reefs. Coral reefs are vital marine habitats that support an array of marine species, including fish, invertebrates, and plants. These reefs also provide essential ecosystem services, such as shoreline protection, carbon sequestration, and tourism opportunities. However, coral reefs are under threat from factors like climate change, ocean acidification, and destructive fishing practices. In response, conservation organizations and local communities are actively engaged in reef restoration projects, coral gardening initiatives, and sustainable fishing practices to preserve these vital ecosystems.

Fiji is also home to unique terrestrial ecosystems, such as rainforests and mangrove forests. These ecosystems play a crucial role in maintaining biodiversity and regulating the climate. Rainforests, with their rich biodiversity, provide habitat for numerous plant and animal species, some of which are found nowhere else on Earth. Mangrove forests, with their dense root systems, act as natural buffers against storm surges and coastal erosion, protecting communities and coastal habitats. Conservation efforts focus on reforestation, habitat restoration, and protected area establishment to conserve these terrestrial ecosystems.

An essential aspect of conservation in Fiji is community engagement and empowerment. Many conservation initiatives are led by local communities who recognize the value of their natural resources and their role as custodians of the land and sea. Traditional management practices, known as "tabu" or "qoliqoli," involve designating certain areas as no-take zones or protected areas to allow marine and terrestrial ecosystems to regenerate and thrive. By involving local communities in conservation decisions, these initiatives not only preserve the environment but also empower communities to take ownership of their natural heritage.

Fiji's commitment to conservation is reflected in the establishment of marine protected areas (MPAs) and national parks. These protected areas play a crucial role in preserving critical habitats, safeguarding endangered species, and promoting sustainable tourism. The Fiji Locally Managed Marine Area Network (FLMMA) is a collaborative effort between government agencies, non-governmental organizations (NGOs), and local communities to manage marine resources sustainably. Through this network, communities are involved in planning and implementing marine conservation strategies that align with their cultural values and livelihoods.

Sustainable tourism is also a key component of conservation efforts in Fiji. The tourism industry in Fiji depends heavily on its natural beauty and ecological diversity. Recognizing this, many resorts and tour operators have adopted eco-friendly practices to minimize their impact on the environment. Sustainable tourism initiatives focus on promoting responsible travel, supporting local communities, and raising awareness about conservation issues among visitors.

The Fijian government plays a pivotal role in conservation through policies and legislation that protect the environment. The Ministry of Environment works alongside NGOs and international partners to address environmental challenges and promote sustainable development. Additionally, Fiji has been active in global initiatives, advocating for climate change mitigation, marine conservation, and sustainable development goals.

Conservation efforts in Fiji are ongoing and dynamic, driven by the collective determination to preserve the country's natural heritage. These efforts not only protect ecosystems and biodiversity but also contribute to the well-being and resilience of local communities. By safeguarding Fiji's ecosystems, we ensure that this island paradise continues to flourish for generations to come, offering its gifts of beauty, wonder, and inspiration to all who embrace its splendor.

Fiji's Economy: Key Industries and Challenges

In the heart of the South Pacific lies Fiji, a nation renowned for its breathtaking beauty and vibrant culture. Behind this picturesque facade lies a diverse economy that plays a pivotal role in the country's development and progress. Fiji's economy is a mix of traditional sectors, modern industries, and a growing emphasis on sustainable practices. As we delve into the intricacies of Fiji's economic landscape, we uncover the key industries that drive the nation's growth and the challenges it faces in navigating a dynamic global economy.

Tourism stands as one of Fiji's primary economic pillars, attracting visitors from all corners of the world to experience the idyllic beaches, crystal-clear waters, and warm hospitality. The tourism industry contributes significantly to Fiji's GDP, provides employment opportunities, and fosters cultural exchange. The country's reputation as a tropical paradise has made it a favored destination for honeymooners, adventure seekers, and nature enthusiasts alike.

Agriculture also plays a vital role in Fiji's economy, with a strong focus on sugarcane production. For many years, sugarcane has been a significant export crop, generating income and employment for thousands of Fijians. Additionally, other agricultural products, such as coconuts, ginger, and tropical fruits, contribute to both domestic consumption and international markets.

The garment and textile industry is another significant player in Fiji's economic landscape, providing employment to a large number of people, particularly women. Many garment factories cater to international brands, benefiting from Fiji's strategic location and preferential trade agreements. However, challenges in the global textile market and increasing competition from other low-cost manufacturing countries pose obstacles to the industry's growth.

Fiji's unique geographical location has also enabled the development of a robust fishing industry. The country's waters teem with an abundance of fish and seafood, making fishing a vital sector for local consumption and export. Sustainable fishing practices are essential to ensure the long-term viability of this industry and preserve the delicate marine ecosystem.

In recent years, Fiji has witnessed the growth of the information technology and outsourcing sector. The availability of a skilled and educated workforce, coupled with government incentives, has attracted international companies to set up business process outsourcing (BPO) centers in the country. This emerging industry has the potential to diversify Fiji's economy further and create new opportunities for its people.

Challenges do exist in Fiji's economic journey. Like many developing nations, Fiji faces the need to balance economic growth with environmental sustainability. Climate change poses a significant threat to Fiji's economy, with rising sea levels and extreme weather events affecting coastal communities, agriculture, and tourism. The nation has been proactive in advocating for climate change mitigation on the global stage, but adaptation strategies and resilience-building remain crucial for safeguarding the economy and the well-being of its citizens.

Investment in education and workforce development is another critical aspect to address challenges in Fiji's economy. Ensuring a skilled and adaptable workforce will empower the nation to embrace technological advancements, diversify industries, and meet the demands of a rapidly evolving global marketplace.

Furthermore, the COVID-19 pandemic brought unprecedented challenges to Fiji's tourism industry, which heavily relies on international visitors. Border closures and travel restrictions significantly impacted the sector, leading to job losses and economic contraction. The government's efforts to balance public health and economic revival will be instrumental in steering Fiji's recovery.

Despite the hurdles, Fiji's economy holds great potential for growth and prosperity. By leveraging its natural beauty, cultural heritage, and strategic location, Fiji can continue to attract investment, foster innovation, and promote sustainable practices. With a strong sense of community and determination, Fiji is poised to overcome challenges and create a thriving economy that benefits all its people.

Tourism in Fiji: Economic Driver and Sustainability

In the enchanting islands of Fiji, tourism weaves a mesmerizing tapestry of cultural diversity, natural splendor, and warm hospitality. As one of the Pacific's most sought-after destinations, tourism plays a central role in Fiji's economy, offering not only economic benefits but also opportunities for cultural exchange and environmental conservation. Let us embark on a journey to unravel the nuances of tourism in Fiji, its impact on the nation's development, and the efforts undertaken to ensure sustainability and responsible practices for the future.

Fiji's allure as a tropical paradise beckons travelers from across the globe, drawn by the promise of idyllic beaches, crystal-clear waters, and a vibrant underwater world. The tourism industry serves as a major economic driver, contributing significantly to Fiji's Gross Domestic Product (GDP) and providing employment opportunities for thousands of Fijians. Hotels, resorts, restaurants, tour operators, and various other businesses thrive on the influx of visitors seeking a taste of paradise.

This influx of tourists brings with it a cultural exchange that enriches both visitors and locals. Travelers are welcomed with the warmth and friendliness that is synonymous with Fijian hospitality, and they are invited to embrace the traditional customs, dance, music, and cuisine that showcase the vibrant Fijian culture. This exchange fosters a deeper understanding and appreciation of different ways of life, bridging gaps and creating lasting connections between people from diverse backgrounds.

However, the allure of Fiji's natural beauty and the popularity of tourism also pose challenges that demand careful consideration. Sustainable tourism practices are crucial to preserve the delicate balance of the environment and culture that make Fiji so enchanting. As a nation that cherishes its pristine landscapes and rich biodiversity, Fiji is deeply committed to safeguarding its natural resources for future generations.

The conservation of Fiji's marine ecosystems is of paramount importance, given the country's extensive coral reefs and diverse marine life. Reefs support numerous species of fish, invertebrates, and other marine creatures, making them a vital component of the underwater ecosystem. Sustainable diving and snorkeling practices, reef restoration projects, and responsible marine tourism initiatives are part of the collective effort to protect these valuable marine habitats. Fiji's commitment to environmental preservation extends beyond the coastline to its lush rainforests and terrestrial ecosystems. Efforts are made to protect and restore forests, creating opportunities for eco-tourism, nature-based experiences, and hiking adventures that immerse visitors in the wonders of Fiji's flora and fauna. By promoting responsible trekking and adhering to Leave No Trace principles, tourism can coexist harmoniously with the natural environment.

The Fijian government, in collaboration with non-governmental organizations (NGOs) and local communities, has embraced the principles of sustainable tourism to ensure that the industry benefits all stakeholders while preserving the nation's natural and cultural heritage. Through initiatives such as the Fiji Ecotourism Policy and the Sustainable Tourism Development Plan, a conscious effort is made to integrate sustainability practices into the fabric of the tourism industry. Community-based tourism is also gaining prominence in Fiji, empowering local communities to actively participate in and benefit from tourism activities. Initiatives like village homestays, cultural tours, and handicraft sales provide an authentic experience for tourists while generating income and supporting the livelihoods of local communities.

In recent times, the COVID-19 pandemic has presented unprecedented challenges to Fiji's tourism industry, with border closures and travel restrictions leading to a sharp decline in international visitors. This period of hardship has reinforced the need for resilience and adaptability, encouraging stakeholders to rethink business models, enhance digital capabilities, and promote domestic tourism to sustain the industry during challenging times.

Tourism in Fiji thrives on the balance between economic prosperity and sustainable practices, ensuring that future generations can continue to experience the splendor of these magical islands. By promoting responsible tourism, fostering cultural understanding, and safeguarding the environment, Fiji embraces a vision of tourism that leaves a positive footprint on the land and hearts of those who visit.

Navigating Fijian Society: Social Issues and Progress

In the vibrant tapestry of Fijian society, tradition and modernity intertwine, shaping the nation's identity and its journey toward progress. As we delve into the complexities of Fijian society, we encounter a diverse array of social issues that demand attention and concerted efforts. Simultaneously, we witness the resilience and determination of the Fijian people to overcome challenges and foster positive change.

Family and community lie at the heart of Fijian culture. The concept of "vanua" emphasizes the strong sense of belonging and interconnectedness among members of a community. Extended families play a pivotal role in providing support and care for their members, fostering a tight-knit network of relationships that serve as a foundation for social stability.

One of the social issues facing Fijian society is gender inequality. Although progress has been made in recent years, traditional gender roles continue to influence societal expectations and opportunities. Women's empowerment and gender equality remain important objectives, with efforts underway to promote women's leadership, access to education, and economic opportunities. Organizations and initiatives advocating for women's rights and gender equity have been instrumental in driving positive change.

Like many nations, Fiji faces challenges related to poverty and income disparity. While the country's economy has experienced growth, disparities between urban and rural areas persist. The government has implemented social welfare programs and poverty alleviation strategies to address these issues, aiming to uplift vulnerable communities and improve their quality of life.

Access to education is a significant area of progress in Fijian society. The government places a strong emphasis on education, offering free primary and secondary education to all citizens. Efforts are ongoing to enhance educational infrastructure, teacher training, and access to tertiary education, providing opportunities for personal development and nurturing a skilled workforce.

Healthcare is another critical aspect of societal progress. The Fijian government is committed to improving healthcare services, particularly in rural and remote areas. Initiatives aim to enhance medical facilities, increase access to healthcare professionals, and combat non-communicable diseases (NCDs) that pose health challenges to the population.

Cultural preservation is an integral part of navigating Fijian society. The richness of Fijian cultural heritage is celebrated through traditional ceremonies, dance, music, and art. Organizations and institutions work diligently to preserve and promote cultural practices, ensuring that they remain cherished and passed down to future generations.

One of the significant social issues in Fiji is the impact of climate change. As a vulnerable island nation, Fiji faces the consequences of rising sea levels, extreme weather events, and changing weather patterns. The Fijian government actively participates in global climate change advocacy, urging collective action to address this pressing global challenge.

Fijian society also grapples with the effects of urbanization and rural-urban migration. As more people move to urban centers seeking better opportunities, there is a need to ensure that cities are equipped to handle population growth while maintaining a balance with rural areas to preserve cultural traditions and heritage.

Community-driven initiatives and social enterprises play a vital role in addressing social issues and fostering progress in Fiji. Many grassroots organizations focus on community development, environmental conservation, women's empowerment, and youth initiatives, reflecting the determination of Fijians to create positive change from within their communities.

The Fijian government, in partnership with civil society and international organizations, continues to work toward creating an inclusive and harmonious society. Policies and programs are designed to address social issues, foster sustainable development, and ensure that the benefits of progress are shared equitably among all Fijians.

Building a Sustainable Future for Fiji

As the sun sets over the tranquil islands of Fiji, a vision of a sustainable future unfolds, where nature and people thrive harmoniously. Fiji stands at a crossroads, balancing the allure of progress with the imperative to safeguard its natural and cultural heritage. In this chapter, we delve into the concerted efforts and initiatives that are paving the way for a sustainable future in Fiji, where economic prosperity, environmental stewardship, and social well-being are intertwined.

Environmental conservation lies at the heart of Fiji's sustainable journey. The nation's abundant natural resources, from pristine beaches to lush rainforests, hold intrinsic value not only for its citizens but also for the world. Fiji's commitment to sustainable practices is evident through its endorsement of the Paris Agreement and its advocacy for climate change action on the global stage. The government has set ambitious targets to reduce greenhouse gas emissions, enhance renewable energy capacity, and implement climate resilience measures.

One of the key components of Fiji's sustainability strategy is eco-tourism. Recognizing that tourism is both an economic driver and a potential threat to the environment, Fiji has taken a proactive approach to promote responsible tourism practices. Eco-lodges, nature-based tours, and sustainable diving initiatives are just a few examples of how Fiji is harnessing its natural beauty to attract visitors while minimizing the ecological footprint of tourism.

Preserving Fiji's marine biodiversity is a top priority, given the importance of healthy coral reefs and diverse marine life to the nation's ecosystem and tourism industry. Efforts to establish marine protected areas, regulate fishing practices, and combat illegal fishing are instrumental in safeguarding Fiji's oceanic treasures for generations to come. Collaboration between the government, local communities, and international organizations ensures that marine conservation remains a collective responsibility.

Land conservation and sustainable agriculture practices are also essential components of Fiji's sustainability framework. By promoting agroforestry, organic farming, and soil conservation techniques, Fiji aims to ensure food security, preserve natural habitats, and reduce the environmental impact of agriculture.

Initiatives to protect and restore forests contribute to carbon sequestration, mitigating the effects of climate change.

Fiji's commitment to renewable energy is evident in its efforts to harness solar, wind, and hydropower resources. The nation has made significant strides in increasing renewable energy capacity and reducing dependence on fossil fuels. Innovative projects such as solar-powered microgrids in remote communities demonstrate the potential of clean energy solutions to improve access to electricity and enhance the resilience of rural areas.

Water conservation is another crucial aspect of Fiji's sustainability agenda. Given the vulnerability of small island nations to water scarcity, Fiji places emphasis on sustainable water management practices, rainwater harvesting, and water conservation awareness campaigns. Protecting freshwater sources and managing water resources efficiently are essential to meet the needs of both communities and ecosystems.

Fiji's commitment to social sustainability is reflected in its focus on inclusive development and empowerment. The government strives to ensure that all citizens have access to education, healthcare, and social services, regardless of their geographic location or socioeconomic status. Social welfare programs, women's empowerment initiatives, and support for vulnerable populations are integral to building a socially just society.

Investment in education and workforce development is central to Fiji's sustainable future. By nurturing a skilled and adaptable workforce, Fiji can embrace technological advancements, diversify industries, and meet the demands of a rapidly evolving global marketplace. Equipping the younger generation with the knowledge and skills to tackle future challenges will be instrumental in securing Fiji's sustainable growth.

Community engagement and collaboration are at the core of Fiji's sustainable development efforts. The involvement of local communities in decision-making processes, environmental stewardship, and sustainable livelihood initiatives ensures that development is rooted in local knowledge, traditions, and needs. Traditional ecological knowledge is valued alongside modern science, creating a holistic approach to sustainability.

Epilogue

As we conclude our exploration of Fiji, we are left in awe of the beauty, diversity, and rich heritage of this island paradise. Throughout our journey, we have immersed ourselves in the history, culture, cuisine, and natural wonders that define Fiji's unique identity.

From the ancient civilizations that once thrived on these islands to the colonial era and struggles for independence, Fiji's history has shaped its present and influenced its path to sovereignty. We have witnessed the resilience and determination of the Fijian people in overcoming challenges and building a harmonious society that cherishes its cultural traditions while embracing modernity.

The breathtaking landscapes of Fiji, from its pristine beaches and lush rainforests to its vibrant coral reefs, captivate the imagination and offer an array of experiences for adventurers and nature enthusiasts alike. The warm hospitality and genuine smiles of the Fijian people welcome visitors from around the world, leaving a lasting impression of the "Bula Spirit" that radiates throughout the islands.

As we indulged in the delectable Fijian cuisine, we discovered a gastronomic journey filled with exotic flavors and fresh ingredients sourced from both land and sea. The fusion of traditional Fijian dishes with influences from various cultures showcased the diversity and creativity that define Fijian culinary arts.

Throughout our exploration, we celebrated the cultural melting pot that is Fiji, where influences from indigenous traditions, colonial legacies, and contemporary global trends coexist harmoniously. The art, music, dance, and storytelling of the Fijian people are a testament to their vibrant cultural heritage and the importance of preserving these treasures for future generations.

We delved into the world of sports and recreation, where rugby stands as a national passion and a symbol of unity. Beyond rugby, Fiji offers an array of recreational activities, from water sports and eco-adventures to traditional games that reflect the spirit of community and celebration.

As we reflected on Fiji's path to a sustainable future, we recognized the nation's dedication to environmental conservation, renewable energy, and responsible tourism. The efforts to protect marine biodiversity, manage water resources, and promote social development epitomize Fiji's commitment to a holistic and inclusive approach to sustainability.

Through our journey, we navigated the complexities of Fijian society, acknowledging both the challenges and progress that shape the nation. Gender equality, poverty alleviation, and access to education and healthcare remain areas of focus, while community-driven initiatives and collaboration pave the way for positive change.

As we bid farewell to Fiji, we carry with us the memories of its picturesque landscapes, the warmth of its people, and the lessons it imparts on sustainability and cultural preservation. Fiji's story is one of resilience, unity, and a steadfast commitment to building a better future for all.

As you close this book, we hope that it has sparked a sense of curiosity and wonder about Fiji's many facets. Whether you dream of exploring its turquoise waters, immersing yourself in its vibrant traditions, or simply savoring the taste of Fijian cuisine, Fiji beckons with open arms, ready to welcome you into its embrace.

As the sun sets on our journey, we extend our heartfelt gratitude to the people of Fiji for sharing their stories, culture, and hospitality with us. May the spirit of "Bula" forever guide your path, and may the enchanting allure of Fiji remain etched in your hearts, inspiring a sense of wonder and appreciation for the marvels of this extraordinary destination.

Until we meet again, "Moce" and farewell from the wondrous islands of Fiji.

Printed in Great Britain
by Amazon

39596432R00056